INTRODUCE you to
JESUS

Published by Barbour Publishing, Inc., P.O. Box 719, Uhrichsville, Ohio 44683 http://www.barbourbooks.com

 Member of the
Evangelical Christian
Publishers Association

Printed in the United States of America.

CONTENTS

PREFACE

"Meeting Jesus is the most important thing that happened to me," Christians will tell you. If you've never met Jesus, you may wonder what they mean. *How can I meet someone who lived years and years ago?* you may ask yourself. *Do I even want to?*

Perhaps a friend has been telling you she's "born again." You wonder if she's gone crazy—or maybe you'd like to have whatever it is that she has, because you can see it's made a huge change in her life. Whatever you've been thinking, you need to know more.

In these pages, I'd like to introduce you to Jesus by showing you what and why Christians believe. We'll consider the core principles of Christianity and why people believe in them.

I'd also like to answer some questions that have probably occurred to you. Who is Jesus really? Why should you listen to those who follow Him? What difference can He make in your life?

Together, let's meet Jesus.

I'D LIKE TO INTRODUCE YOU TO
JESUS

PAMELA MCQUADE

BARBOUR
PUBLISHING, INC.
Uhrichsville, Ohio

Part I

WHO IS THIS JESUS?

1

JESUS WHO?

Who do others say Jesus is?
Here's what the world will tell you.

"Who do you think Jesus is?" Go out on the street, take a poll, and you'll get a variety of answers to the question. Some people will merely give you a confused look, others may launch into a diatribe against Jesus, and another group will give you reasoned opinions—though those opinions will come in all shapes and sizes.

Anyone can have an opinion of Jesus. The agnostic college professor who continually challenges Christian students. . .the farmer who tells others that his

success is based on his faith in Jesus, the Son of God. . .
the businessman. . .the teacher. . .the factory worker
. . .each person is free to have a personal view on Jesus
Christ.

With all these differing views of Jesus around,
which one do you believe? Is the doubting college professor correct? Or is the believing farmer on the right
track, the one who has been through so many tough
times? Do we trust the professor's years of education—
or the farmer's lifetime of everyday hardship?

Does it even matter what you think? Is there a
"right" answer to the question?

Making the Right Decision

The most popular viewpoint regarding faith in Jesus
is that every person has a right to his or her own view;
all views are valid, because everything depends on
your perspective. But how can both the farmer and
professor be right? Is there a right and wrong to faith?

If you've ever been on a jury in a court of law, you
know that a court case can't have two "right" decisions. You can't say the defendant is both guilty and

innocent. Obviously, each person will have his or her own perspective on any set of circumstances, but most people still accept that there is such a thing as truth. In other words, there is a right and a wrong answer.

But when we come to the spiritual world, many people reject the idea that there is such a thing as absolute, verifiable truth. Faith, according to this way of thinking, is a vague belief system. As "practical" people of the twenty-first century, we may feel as though spiritual faith asks us to leave behind the solid ground of logic and concrete thinking while we step off into an unsubstantiated haze. No wonder faith seems irrelevant to so many folks.

But plenty of people have found that their faith was born when they took a look at Christianity in a more practical light. These people considered the truth of the case. They asked questions of the eyewitnesses and listened carefully to their evidence. Like jurors searching for the right verdict, they uncovered the truth to make a "right" decision—and they were not left floating in the haze.

When you look at Jesus as if you were a juror in court, you have to consider the evidence—as we'll do in the following chapters. This is a case with lots of testimony and facts, more than can be contained in one small book. But we'll at least find the point where you can start your research of the case. If you need more evidence before you make your decision, the Suggested Reading list at the end of the book offers sources that will go into these issues more fully.

A Question of Bias

One thing courts deal with up front is the issue of biases and how they can influence the outcome of a trial. After a brief outline of the case, a judge asks prospective jurors if anything would keep them from fairly evaluating the case. Jurors who have had a child addicted to drugs might not be able to set aside their feelings on a drug case. If the case concerns a man who is accused of abusing his wife, a woman who has been abused herself is probably not going to see the verdict as clearly as one who has never been harmed.

We all come into any situation with our own set of biases. Based on our past experiences, we tend to think certain ways about any subject—whether it's how to vote in the next election or what kind of spiritual commitment we should have.

Before we decide what to believe about Jesus, we need to understand our biases and how they will impact our decision. We'll start with a look at the biases and attitudes of the people who want to tell you who Jesus really is. Once we understand the basis of our attitudes, we can begin to make a fair evaluation of what we think and why we think it—then we can ask ourselves if what we are thinking is correct.

Who Is Jesus?

When you boil it all down, there aren't a lot of different ways to think about Jesus. Non-Christian descriptions or attitudes about this controversial man predictably fall into three categories:

- He's a good man
- He's a fraud
- He doesn't matter

What do each of these perspectives contribute to the case for or against Jesus?

He's a Good Man

Based on the descriptions of Jesus that appear in the Bible, many people will at least admit that He was a good man. After all, He did good for others, and He took on the hypocritical religious establishment. You have to say something nice about Him. "Good man" covers the bases without committing yourself too much.

People began saying this when Jesus was on earth. The Bible reports: "When Jesus entered Jerusalem, the whole city was stirred and asked, 'Who is this?' The crowds answered, 'This is Jesus, the prophet from Nazareth in Galilee' "(Matthew 21:10–11).

This testimony of many people who had heard about Jesus, maybe even those who had seen Him a time or two, was basically a "He's a good man" comment. They had seen that He did kind things. He even did miraculous things. Obviously an ordinary man could not perform the miracles He had done, so the crowds were willing to believe that He had some connection with God. They called Him a prophet, but they weren't willing to go any further. And they were right: Jesus did prophesy.

You don't have to be a Christian to believe Jesus was a prophet. Today, Islam accepts Jesus as a prophet, while rejecting His divinity. The central ideas of Christianity, including sin, salvation, and the certainty of eternal life, are not Islamic teachings. Like many in first-century Jerusalem's crowd, Islam considers Jesus to be, at best, a good man.

But was a man who did what Jesus did *only* a prophet? When we look in Chapter 3 at the claims Jesus made for Himself, we'll see He said He was a lot more that that.

Not everyone who describes Jesus as a good man, however, will want to go so far as to call Him "prophet." Perhaps for some the term is unfamiliar; others may not want to ascribe that much power to this remarkable man. But some concepts about Jesus appear to give Him a limited amount of acceptance. Hindus, with their hundreds of gods, can recognize Jesus' goodness simply by adding Him to the rest of their deities. But since Hindus, unlike Christians, also believe that everyone and everything is God, when they accept Jesus as a god, they're not setting Him above the rest of humanity.

None of the "good man" views accept Jesus as

Christians do, as the one true God, the Savior who died for our sins.

He's a Fraud

Others believe that Jesus was a fraud. Some figure out elaborate plots in which the disciples tried to hide the "truth" of the Resurrection. These fraud proclaimers often devise elaborate ideas about how the apostles—who for the most part were men with limited education and resources—could have fooled a world that was highly critical of the man they proclaimed as God. In Chapter 2, we'll take a look at how believable their ideas are.

> **Apostle:** Meaning "one who is sent out." This title was applied to the twelve disciples whom Jesus hand-picked to follow Him and help with His ministry. Judas, one of the original twelve, eventually betrayed Jesus (Mark 3:16–19). The other disciples later chose Matthias to replace Judas, but today we often think of Paul as the twelfth apostle.
> **Disciple:** a follower of Jesus.

Another way of proclaiming Jesus is a fraud is to look for the so-called "historical" Jesus. Those who argue for this "theology" seem to ignore the historical evidence, not accepting the evidence of those who were eyewitnesses to the life and ministry of Jesus. Instead they begin by discounting anything miraculous in the Bible. You might say they start by ignoring any testimonies that do not fit in with their theory. Such people are sure to fulfill the quip, "There are no miracles to those who do not believe in them."

If Jesus was a liar, a con man, and therefore an evil, foolish man, then how can we explain that He left us with the most profound moral instruction and powerful moral example that anyone has ever left?[1]

One group seeking the "historical Jesus," the Jesus Seminar, has voted on the accuracy of Jesus' sayings. This group has decided that only 2 percent of Jesus' sayings were His actual words.[2] Apparently, they put their ultimate faith in the power of the vote: People who were not eyewitnesses, who lived two thousand years after the biblical events and half a world away from the places where they occurred, have claimed for themselves the authority to say what really happened.

He Doesn't Matter

A Buddhist in search of God needs to begin by finding a religion, because strictly speaking, Buddhism is a philosophy of life, not a religion. This offshoot of Hinduism deals with suffering and how to avoid it. Buddha never claimed to be a prophet or incarnation of God; he simply sought to lead others to "enlightenment." In Buddhism, Jesus does not matter because Buddhism:

- Does not affirm the reality of God
- Denies the reality of evil
- Does not acknowledge a "self" to sin or be forgiven through a Savior

Others who declare that Jesus does not matter are those who lack a formal "theology"; for various reasons, they do not like to be confronted with many

Christian concepts. Some are involved in wrongdoing they know the Bible condemns: The adulterer usually doesn't want to hear he must change his ways and love his family; the thief does not want to hear he should not steal.

We all have things in our lives that we don't want Jesus or anyone else to confront. So even if we're "good people," we may tend to write off Christian doctrine. What it comes down to, finally, is that Jesus doesn't matter because *we* do—we want to be in charge of our own lives and do as we please. We aren't keen on something Jesus says, so we say He's not important. We don't hear what we don't want to hear.

To be the ultimate rulers of our own lives, we have to act as if Jesus' words don't matter. To put it another way, we say He is a liar—He's not really what He says He is—so we don't need to listen. If Jesus' claims are not real, there is no sin and no need to be saved from it, no hellfire or judgment—all things Jesus *did* talk about. But if Jesus' claims are not true, all's right with the world—or at least as right as we think we can expect it to be.

Agnostics or atheists also discount Jesus. They say God can't be known or doesn't exist; either way, He would never interfere with our lives.

If what Jesus taught isn't true or doesn't matter, then He doesn't matter either. There's no need to pay attention to Him. We can do as we please, ruling our own worlds. "I can do as I want, as long as I don't hurt anyone" is often the catch phrase of this group of doubters. "Jesus doesn't matter" believers will tell you that all religions are equal. Believe in this or that; either way, everything will turn out fine.

If these folk have any concept of Jesus, they might relate to the people in Jesus' hometown. Confronted with His claims, the townspeople responded, "Is this not Jesus, the son of Joseph, whose father and mother we know? How can he now say, 'I came down from heaven'?" (John 6:42). The Jesus they expected was the small child in the manger or the young boy visiting Jerusalem—familiar and unthreatening figures who didn't expect much of them. But they did not accept the claims of the adult Jesus. Many people today are much the same. They're comfortable with the familiar Christmas image of a pretty baby in a quaint manger, but they're uneasy with a Man whose claims might threaten the way they live their lives.

Is Belief in Jesus Crazy?

There are minor variations on these three views of Jesus. Some who hold them may be part of a religion other than Christianity, others may belong to a cult, and still others are "independent" thinkers who unknowingly fall into one or another of these categories. Each has an opinion about Jesus. None believe in the Jesus the Bible describes at such length. Are any of them right? Is faith in Jesus crazy? What can you believe with confidence?

No matter who is talking about Jesus, each person has a preconceived idea about Him. Past experiences, biases, and religious systems that are not Christian may all feed into the mix that has caused the opinion. To judge how a person approaches Him, we need to understand his or her past beliefs. Perhaps the professor saw hypocritical Christians as a child and has written Christianity off because of it. Perhaps the farmer came from a strong family of faith—or maybe he saw some other evidence that caused him to believe.

Many non-Christians will give you the idea that faith in Jesus is illogical or simpleminded. You'd never feel comfortable admitting you were considering Jesus, because you'd fear their ridicule. But how many of them have really looked into the claims of Jesus? How many can tell you why many brilliant people, and many ordinary ones, have a strong faith that this man was the Son of God?

Sooner or later, there is a discussion. . .about the Bible. Nearly always someone comments on all the contradictions in it. . .I have a suspicion that the vast majority of people who say that have never read the Bible thoroughly. A Bible is often treated like a dictionary—most homes have one, but hardly anyone ever uses it.[3]

Maybe the most logical question you need to ask yourself is this: "If they don't believe in Jesus, what do they believe?" And the corollary might be: "What is their unbelief based on?"

The Importance of Belief

Whether or not you realize it, you build your life on beliefs. Some, like the fact that you are sitting in a chair or living in your home, have a concrete, physically provable aspect. Others, like the fact that your parents, spouse, or friends love you, are more difficult to demonstrate. But we all have some beliefs, even if we only believe that we don't believe something. People who say "I don't believe in Jesus" may be Muslims, Buddhists, or atheists, but each has a set of beliefs of some sort. Everyone believes *something*.

> **It is never a question with any of us of faith or no faith; the question always is, "In what or in whom do we put our faith?"**
>
> **Anonymous**

Non-Christians may make an emotional case for not believing in Jesus. For instance, they may say, "I can't believe in a good God who would allow evil in the world." Or they may make a logical argument: "How could a dead person rise to life?" But have they sought real answers for their questions and looked at both sides of the evidence? Often, they haven't.

A Logical Response to Non-Christians

Whether the case against Jesus is being made from an emotional or a rational point of view, one has to look at the logic behind any view of Jesus. Can anyone reasonably call Jesus a good man, fraud, or someone who simply does not matter?

As the author C. S. Lewis shows, there really aren't many logical options for what to make of Jesus. Like the Jews of Jesus' day, when they come face to face with the Jesus who lives in the Bible, modern-day doubters may discover He's not what they expected.

> **A man who was merely a man and said the sort of things Jesus said. . .would either be a lunatic—on a level with the man who says he is a poached egg—or else he would be the Devil of Hell. You must make your choice. Either this man was, and is, the Son of God: or else a madman or something worse.[4]**

Amazingly, though many people have attacked Jesus in many ways, you'd be hard pressed to find someone who claimed that Jesus was a lunatic. Even people who would fight to the death the idea that

Jesus was the Son of God may still find His teachings inspiring or good. No one seriously claims they were the ideas of a madman.

The personality of Jesus and the power of his message point to a profound sanity.[5]

Do you have to give up either brains or emotional sanity to believe in Jesus? No. Many highly intelligent people who have carefully considered the evidence have come to believe in Jesus as the Christ. Nor did they become emotionally disturbed because of their choice.

Charles Colson read C. S. Lewis's defense of the Christian faith, *Mere Christianity*, and suddenly saw the emptiness of his own life. In his book *Born Again*, this tough guy of the Nixon White House describes how, when he became a Christian, he put behind him the ruthlessness that had brought him to high office, then destroyed his life.

Josh McDowell, challenged to read the evidence for Christianity, determined to write a book to disprove it. Instead of disproving the faith, Josh's studies brought him to the realization that he didn't have a leg to stand on. Eventually, he too became a Christian.[6]

Both men have had successful careers in Christian missions. They aren't madmen, though they are men with a commitment. They've won respect in their fields and have shown others that you don't have to put aside your intellects in order to believe in Christ.

Making a Wise Decision

So who is right? The people who call Jesus a good man, a fraud, or someone who really doesn't matter? Or are C. S. Lewis, Charles Colson, and Josh McDowell right?

To help you make a wise decision, in the chapters ahead we'll look at some of the ideas and information thoughtful Christians have considered before making their decision to believe in Christ. We'll also consider some passages from the Bible that provide three testimonies:

• What Jesus said about Himself

- What His closest friends, the apostles, said
  of Him
- What the Old Testament said about the Messiah

Then we'll take a quick look at the early church
to see what those people believed.

These testimonies will help answer the question,
"Who is this Jesus?"

2

THE GOSPEL TESTIMONY

What did eyewitnesses say about Jesus?

Imagine yourself in a court of law, about to hear a case concerning a theft that took place in New York City. What would you think if one of the lawyers brought as a witness a man who had never left China until his court appearance, had never known the plaintiff or defendant, but had read an account in the newspaper? You'd probably have a lot of questions about why the lawyer was using this man as a witness. "Wouldn't it be better," you might ask, "to talk to the people who owned the home that was robbed? How about the neighbors, or even the policemen who came to the scene of the crime?"

When you ask those questions, you're asking for primary sources. To historians, a primary source is an eyewitness account, or at least the account of someone who was alive at the time the events occurred. This is the best kind of historical evidence you can get.

For many well-accepted events in history, the primary sources are limited. In some cases, especially when we're dealing with ancient history, we may only have the testimony of a single person. Not many ancient eyewitness accounts are still in existence. Sometimes the best account available comes from a hundred or more years after the event. But if these accounts are based on information from a person who saw what happened, most historians consider their record to be acceptable. The further a source is from the actual events, the more you have to question the record's accuracy.

The Testimony About Jesus

When we look at Jesus' story, we do not have to rely on a single primary source; we have the four Gospels.

All four accounts are told by men who either knew Jesus personally or were compiling the stories of eyewitnesses to His life.

These eyewitnesses had spent time with Jesus for at least three years. They heard His words and saw His actions. They didn't have to guess what happened, which words He spoke and which He didn't. These people were there, and we have the Gospels that record their experiences; we also have the letters they wrote to the early church, carefully copied for centuries.

In historical terms, these are topnotch sources. If you were trying to write a biography, the apostles are just the sort of people you'd want to go to for documentation. But most folks don't have numerous accounts recorded of their lives, or if they do, these documents do not get passed down for more than a brief time. In fact, few lives are as well testified to as that of Jesus.

A book written by, say, a twentieth-century theologian who discounts the report of a Gospel writer is far from being a primary source. The writer was not there. He or she may make some assumptions about what happened, but the burden of proof will always be on that scholar to show that the primary text is in error.

Hastily accepting this scholar's outlook is like accepting an opinion from the man from China about what went on at that crime scene we mentioned at the beginning of the chapter. There might be a chance that the fellow from China was right about what happened, but he'd have to have unusual information to make his story credible—and you'd especially doubt his testimony if it went against the descriptions of the eyewitnesses. So when a scholar begins to doubt the Gospel testimonies, be sure that person makes a watertight case, not one simply based on a non-Christian worldview or emotion.

Before we go further, let's take a look at our primary sources: Matthew, Mark, Luke, and John.

Giving the Gospels a Fair Hearing

We want to give the Gospels a fair hearing, one in which we carefully consider the people who are giving the testimony and the situation in which they wrote. People who read the Gospels (and other ancient sources) often consider them from a prideful point of view. We often believe that the way we think today or the things we believe in our culture are the best and only way to look at the world. We discount the testimonies from other eras by treating them as if they were irrational and unintelligent.

Frequently, we imagine that because we live in a "scientific age," we can judge things better. We assume that people who have less education than we do or did not have light bulbs to illuminate their homes have nothing to say to us.

True, most of the men who wrote down the testimonies we will consider did not have a formal education equivalent to today's college degree. Their homes did not have electric lights or running water. But do not make the mistake of thinking they were not very bright. By attentively reading their accounts, you can see that these are not stupid people. They give a careful account of what occurred and have insight into the thoughts and feelings of others. And some of them had received the best education their day could offer.

Why do we call the Bible "Holy Scripture"?

**The Bible is the "Holy Scripture" because God the
Holy Spirit gave to His chosen writers the thoughts that
they expressed and the words that they wrote (verbal
inspiration). Therefore, the Bible is God's own Word and
truth, without error (inerrancy).[7]**

Consider the testimony of the Gospel writers'
contemporaries. Though the Sanhedrin, Israel's religious rulers, considered Peter and John "unschooled,
ordinary men," their courage astonished the rulers,
and they "took note that these men had been with
Jesus" (Acts 4:13). The disciples had learned valuable lessons in the three years they followed their
Master. Obviously the formally educated leaders of
their day considered them a force to be reckoned
with.

These rulers might have considered Peter and
John rough and unsophisticated, but they did not try
to discount the apostles' testimony by labeling them
foolish or stupid. How easily they might have dis-
counted the apostles' claims by making such statements! But perhaps the Jewish leaders knew this
would be a useless tactic because there had been so

many eyewitnesses to the risen Jesus. In any event, the leaders of Jerusalem did not criticize the intelligence or sanity of the men who proclaimed the Resurrection.

New Testament Reliability

We may accept that the people who wrote the New Testament were not dumb—but is the New Testament reliable? Many scholars have asked this. They have probed and prodded the text, studied its words and sentence construction, and asked questions about every bit of content. They have compared the New Testament to accounts of other authors of the same period and asked questions about the people who wrote Scripture.

What other ancient text has been so picked and pulled at? If another text were so used and abused, what would be left of it? Why, after years of critical pummeling, is this book still a force to be reckoned with? Why hasn't it already been disproved?

Manuscript Evidence

One of the reasons that the Bible is still with us is that no other ancient text has been so carefully preserved. Though individual tallies may vary, scholars judge that well more than 5,600 Greek manuscripts of the New Testament exist today—and that does not count the Latin Vulgate copies or those in other languages. Though not all 5,600 are complete documents, each still testifies to a portion of the New Testament.[8] No other ancient written work has as many manuscripts to document its writing.

The Roman historian Livy wrote the *History of Rome* about A.D. 30, and this book is attested to by twenty manuscripts, a far cry from the New Testament's more than 5,000; yet scholars have never cast doubts on Livy's work. Compare the state of the New Testament manuscripts and those of Livy's history: Only thirty-five of the 142 books in Livy's history are intact—of the remaining 107, two are missing entirely, and only fragments remain of the rest.[9] Not only are passages missing; most of the extant copies of Livy's work were made nine centuries after it was written. By contrast, the first complete New Testament manuscript is documented around A.D. 325, 225 years after the original authors' work.[10]

> Scholars are far from unanimous about the actual date of the first Christian writing. . . . Recent theories include such early dates as the mid-30s for Matthew or late A.D. 44 for Mark. It is now certain that the oral tradition was being written down at a much earlier stage than previously assumed. . . . Clement of Alexandria may well have been correct when he corroborated the tradition that Peter was still alive when Mark's gospel was written and that it was written in Rome.[11]

Remember that manuscripts were laboriously copied by hand throughout this period. The more copying that occurred, the more likely changes were to appear in the text. No doubt a modern copy of Livy's history is more likely to have errors than the books of Matthew, Mark, Luke, and John. There were fewer originals to compare it to, and after 900 years, it could be far from the original.

Then why does the New Testament receive such critical questioning? Perhaps it is a good thing that the New Testament has been so prodded and poked.

After all, few folks are likely to set their life course on the works of Livy. Even those who study the philosophical works of Plato do not entrust their lives to it with the kind of commitment that faith in Jesus demands. It is only fair that when a person considers the claims of Jesus, the study should be rigorous.

The Gospel Accounts

In the Gospels, four different writers, with different views and backgrounds, give us a picture of what Jesus was like, what He did, and how people responded to Him. Who are the men who transcribed these accounts? What are their differences and similarities? How reliable are they? What do their accounts mean to Scripture?

Matthew

When Matthew met Jesus, Matthew was well on his way to a wonderful career as a tax collector. This was not exactly a great career move for a Jew—Matthew was working for the Romans, who had conquered his nation, and other Jews hated him for it. Tax collectors not only demanded the tax payment the Romans required; in order to live well, they added money on top of that for their living expenses. And tax collectors, like most of us, did not want to live in a low-income bracket. The average tax collector probably figured that if he was going to have a job that made everyone hate him, he might as well get wealthy at it—and most did just that by demanding exorbitant payments from their fellow Jews. Honesty just wasn't their policy.

The book has been called "the Gospel according to Matthew" since A.D. 125.... An alternative of any sort to a single author or compiler, Matthew or Levi, which can truly command acceptance, cannot, on present evidence, be advanced.[12]

Maybe Matthew was tired of tax collecting—the life he was leading wasn't all it was cracked up to be. At any rate, when Jesus called him from his tax-collecting booth, Matthew went immediately (Matthew 9:9). No ifs, ands, or buts.

Matthew's life, before he met Jesus, was hardly squeaky clean. But when he gives his testimony in the next verses (9:10–12), he gives an honest account. The new disciple tells of a party Jesus came to at his house. Matthew had invited a crowd of his friends— probably many other tax collectors—to meet Jesus. When the religious Pharisees saw this, they took Jesus' disciples to task. How could Jesus eat with such "sinners"? they wanted to know.

How many of us, writing about ourselves, would rush to tell people of our most embarrassing moments? If, as some would like to contend of the early Christians, we were trying to sell people a line, we'd make sure no one had a clue that we had some dishonesty in our past.

That's one of the amazing things about the Bible. People don't come off as flawless. Matthew is not the only one who tells of his own bad decisions. If the apostles had been trying to pull off a fraud, how likely is it that they'd share moments that made them look bad? Yet in both the Old and New Testaments, some "worst moments" are described: David's illicit relationship with Bathsheba (2 Samuel 11–12), the near destruction of his kingdom by David's son Absalom (2 Samuel 13–20), Peter's failure of faith in the hours before the Crucifixion (Matthew 26:69–75; Mark

14:66–72), and the near riot that came as a result of Paul's efforts to preach to the Jews in Thessalonica (Acts 17:5–9).

Despite his less-than-perfect life, Matthew came to appreciate his own Jewishness. His Gospel links the Old and New Testaments by concentrating on Jesus as the Messiah—the long-expected Savior the prophets had foretold. Though he may have spent years working against his own people, Matthew certainly had knowledge of the Jewish Scriptures. He refers to the Old Testament more than any other Gospel writer. Matthew heard Jesus' words, saw His acts, and compared them with the Old Testament. Then he gave his testimony to the Jews that Jesus was their long-expected Messiah and supported it out of their own Scriptures.

The widely-held, but unsubstantiated, present-day hypothesis that Matthew copied from Mark's Gospel is, on the face of it, absurd. It is not at all certain that Mark even knew Jesus. . . . Why should Matthew have to copy from one who had not been an eyewitness of things that he himself had seen with his own eyes and had heard over and over with his own ears?[13]

Matthew also provides us with ten parables that are not in the other gospels.[14] Thus we can see the importance of multiple gospels describing the life and ministry of Jesus. The Gospel writers tell the same story, but just as four of your friends might tell of your life and describe different moments in it, Matthew, Mark, Luke, and John related to Jesus differently and were struck by different points in His ministry. By combining the testimony of all four authors, we have a more complete picture of Him.

Mark

Though he had contact with both the apostles Paul and Peter, Mark is not one of the twelve disciples first called by Jesus. Some Bible scholars surmise that Mark was the young man who fled, leaving his garment behind, when Jesus was arrested (Mark 14:51–52). But even if Mark was not with Jesus just before His trial and crucifixion, John Mark is an often-mentioned member of the early Christian community.

Peter's listeners were spiritually enlightened by his preaching—so much so that they were not satisfied with just a single hearing. . . . They wanted more than

unwritten teaching of God's word, so they persistently
sought out Mark. . . . They exhorted Mark to leave them
a written statement of the teaching. . . . They didn't quit
until he was persuaded. . . .[15]

Papias (A.D. 140) and Irenaeus (A.D. 175), a disciple of the apostle John, connected Mark's Gospel
with the apostle Peter. As Peter gave his testimony to
the church, Mark compiled it. By writing down the
experiences of the apostle, Mark shared Peter's testimony with the entire church. This, the shortest
Gospel, is believed by scholars to be the first written
account of Jesus' life.

Moving with a rapid pace and focusing on the
miraculous in Jesus' ministry, Mark's account would
appeal to a Roman audience, to whom it was origi-
nally addressed according to early church tradition.
The fact that he uses Latin words and explains the
customs of the Jews supports that tradition. Another
indicator that he writes for Romans is that though he
is called "John Mark" in the Book of Acts and the
Epistles, for the purposes of this Gospel, the writer
uses only his Latin name: Mark.

One of the issues that often comes up when the

New Testament is being discussed is the authorship and dating of the Gospels. From the distance of many hundreds of years, some scholars in the past couple of centuries have attempted to cast doubt on the authorship of the Gospels. But the early church accepted Matthew or Levi, Jesus' disciple; Mark or John Mark, Peter's companion; and Luke, companion to Paul, as the authors of these books. According to biblical scholar Craig L. Blomberg, historically: "There are no known competitors for these three gospels [Matthew, Mark, and Luke]. Apparently, it was just not in dispute." He explains that an unclear reference by Papias to the authorship of this Gospel has caused some confusion, but the early church identified John, son of Zebedee, as the author of the Book of John.[16] Irenaeus confirms that John, the disciple of Jesus who leaned on his breast, wrote the Gospel.[17]

Papias says that Mark, at Peter's insistence, wrote down accurately, though not necessarily chronologically, what Peter remembered of Christ's words and doings.[18]

Mark is estimated by some scholars to have been written between A.D. 50–70. In this era, surely the church would have been filled with people who knew the apostles. These men and women would have known about Peter's ministry and they would have known who was helping him. They would have been aware of a companion who recorded a testimony meant to be shared with the church. If a question about the authorship existed, people of the next generation, like Papias and John's disciple Irenaeus, would probably have been aware of any shocking fallacies. Without a doubt, they would have spoken clearly against it.

Doubting the testimony of the early church as to the authorship of the Gospels is a bit like expecting the man from China to know what happened in New York.

Luke

Historians love the Book of Luke. Here before them is the gospel story, laid out in a direct line, with historically identifiable facts and places. Luke draws a map of the ancient world in Jesus' life and ministry, and in the Book of Acts, continues westward with the growing church.

Luke, the only Gentile writer in the New Testament, was not a disciple of Jesus until after the Resurrection. Though Luke often tells of Paul's travels, it is not until Acts 16:10 that he refers indirectly to himself: "We got ready at once to leave for Macedonia." Scholars conclude that at this point Luke joined the missionary trips of the apostle.

Luke's is the 'Pauline' Gospel, stressing the universality of the message, racial tolerance, the wide place of women.[19]

Though Luke did not personally see Jesus' ministry, his Gospel offers many intimate details. To him we owe knowledge of Mary's feelings when the angel approached her: "Mary was greatly troubled at his words" (Luke 1:29). He tells of Mary's visit to her cousin Elizabeth and records Mary's psalm of praise, the Magnificat, and he tells of the presentation of Jesus at the temple. Obviously Luke had spoken to Mary, who trusted him enough to share personal moments in her life.

Throughout the Gospel, Luke has clearly been careful about his documentation. "Many have undertaken

to draw up an account of the things that have been fulfilled among us, just as they were handed down to us
by those who from the first were eyewitnesses and ser-
vants of the word," he comments. "Therefore, since I
myself have carefully investigated everything from the
beginning, it seemed good also to me to write an
orderly account for you" (Luke 1:1–3). A close reading
of the Gospel confirms that Luke was faithful to his
intention. His account is bursting with details concerning the people and places involved in Jesus' ministry.

Luke's account has been questioned by scholars
who have doubted his accuracy concerning places,
word usage, and references to people. But time and
again, archeology has proved Luke reliable. Says
Steve Kumar, "Archeology. . .has proven the accuracy
of Luke's writings at every point where it is possible
to verify."[20]

British archeologist Sir William Ramsay (1851–
1939), following the liberal German theology of the
nineteenth century, believed that the Book of Acts
had been written two centuries after Christ's death.
Ramsey went to Asia Minor, determined to disprove
Luke's writings. Instead, he found so much of the
biblical text confirmed that his beliefs changed.

He determined that the New Testament clearly described the second half of the first century after Christ. On the basis of his study, he became a firm believer in the Scriptures' accuracy.

John

The first three Gospels are often called the Synoptic Gospels. *Synoptic* means "seeing together," and the first three Gospels are very similar, telling a somewhat chronological narrative, though they include different stories and have different outlooks.

But even a careless reader can see that the Book of John is different from the other testaments to Jesus' ministry. This Gospel begins with a glorious view of Jesus, the Word, in eternity. John, "the disciple whom Jesus loved" (John 13:23), does not follow the clear chronology of the earlier Gospels. Instead he aims to show readers that Jesus was the Son of God by including some of Jesus' lengthy discourses. Unlike the other Gospel authors, John does not record Jesus' parables, focusing instead on what Jesus said about Himself.

> John writes as a witness to Jesus. Again and again
> the reader is confronted with claims that demand a
> verdict. John draws contrasts between life and death,
> faith and unbelief, and the reader is urged to choose.[21]

Traditionally the Book of John was reported to
be written at the end of the first century, from A.D.
80–100, but some scholars have posited an earlier
date, perhaps even as early as the fifties.[22] Biblical
research has supported first-century dates for all the
Gospels. Scholars may disagree about exactly what
decade the Gospel accounts were written, but the
evidence points to an era when the apostles or their
disciples were living.

Unlike today's literate society, in the first century
many people often could not read, and they had little
access to written materials. There was no moveable
type to print multiple copies with ease. The written
word was less commonly used than the oral tradition,
in which people recounted stories over and over for an
audience. The apostles often told their stories, which
would have kept the accounts clear in their memories
for many years. Those who listened would also remain
familiar with their good news.

Were you doing research in another area of ancient history, the Gospels would be considered excellent documentation. Even if you considered John as the last Gospel and dated it in the last part of the first century, it would be much more reliable than later objections. At the end of the first century, people who knew the apostles and had heard their accounts were still alive. Historically, not much had been lost, and enough time had not gone by for tall tales and myths to develop around Jesus.

Responding to the Critics

Critics of the Scriptures will point out that the Gospels, too, are biased. Of course! No one can write without a bias of some sort. But in the four Gospels, you don't have to read far to identify the bias. Each writer points it out to readers:

> Matthew records the genealogy of Jesus, through Joseph, then declares: "Thus there were fourteen generations in all from Abraham to David, fourteen from David to the exile to Babylon, and fourteen from the

exile to the Christ [Jesus]" (Matthew 1:17).

Mark begins his Gospel: "The beginning of the gospel about Jesus Christ, the Son of God" (Mark 1:1).

Luke explains, "Therefore, since I myself have carefully investigated everything from the beginning, it seemed good also to me to write an orderly account for you, most excellent Theophilus, so that you may know the certainty of the things you have been taught" (Luke 1:3–4).

"But these are written," John tells his readers, at the end of his Gospel, "that you may believe that Jesus is the Christ, the Son of God, and that by believing you may have life in his name" (John 20:31).

All four authors are upfront about their intentions. They want to describe the life of Jesus Christ, God's Son. There is no hidden agenda here.

What is Christianity?
Christianity is the life and salvation God has given in and through Jesus Christ.[23]

Some seek to discount the Gospel accounts, claiming they are too biased. They seem to be saying that to be a trustworthy eyewitness, one cannot have a bias. But where can we find this unbiased person? Certainly not in the middle of a controversial situation. Perhaps their "unbiased" person will have lived hundreds of years later. But if scholars seek to trust a later source, they are giving up the accuracy of the eyewitness account. Their preferred source may not have a strong opinion on the subject, but perhaps that's because he or she knows too little to make a judgment. Again, it's like the man from China giving testimony. That fellow is probably pretty objective about the crime that took place in New York—but he's bound to be fairly ignorant of the details as well.

When it comes to describing Jesus, you can accept the accounts of the Gospel writers or you can listen instead to the opinions of the men who wanted to destroy Him—the spiritual leaders of His day. You could hardly say that they were unbiased, but theirs is the only first-century, eyewitness alternative testimony that remains to scholars. (We'll look at their bias in the next chapter.)

The Gospels are still the most complete documents we have that describe Jesus. And their testimony still stands after two thousand years. Read what they have to say for yourself, secure in the fact that you can believe the accounts of these four men.

3

JESUS IN HIS OWN WORDS

What did Jesus say about Himself?

Remember what C. S. Lewis said: "A man who was merely a man and said the sort of things Jesus said. . . would either be a lunatic—on a level with the man who says he is a poached egg—or else he would be the Devil of Hell."[24] C. S. Lewis didn't give us many options, did he? But was he right? What did Jesus really say about Himself? Did He say anything that would indicate He was crazy? Or are we dealing with a horribly wicked man instead? Could it just be possible He really is who He said He is?

Did I Hear That Right?

Much of the four Gospels is made up of Jesus' sayings: parables He told, directions to the disciples, and so on. But some of the most revealing comments are those Jesus made about Himself. These are not the ordinary daily conversations you might share with your friends. In fact, if one of your friends started saying the things Jesus said, you'd be taking him to a counselor to check out his problem.

If the Pharisees and Sadducees could have, they might have wanted to take Jesus to someone to check out His sanity. Imagine the situation from their perspective: A man comes into town and makes some terrifying claims. First He claims, "The kingdom of God is near. Repent and believe the good news!" (Mark 1:15). That must have caused Israel's leaders to wonder. Why hadn't they, the spiritual leaders of the country, been the first to know about this? Did it really take some upstart to let them in on what God was doing? They hardly thought so. Worse, shortly after that, this new prophet was joined by followers whom he promised to make "fishers of men" (Mark 1:17). Obviously, the leaders had a real problem on their hands. Before this thing expanded, they had to get it under control.

But still worse was to come for the Pharisees and Sadducees. While Jesus welcomed people such as prostitutes and tax collectors, He began to attack the religious leaders—men who spent all their days trying to follow every law the Jewish faith had. Apparently, Jesus didn't like the rules they'd added to Scripture. And He wasn't impressed by their efforts to get points with God.

In the course of His ministry, Jesus made some damning statements about Israel's religious leadership. He condemned them for:

- Unrighteousness (Matthew 5:20).
- Following all the rules made by men but neglecting God (Luke 11:42).
- Hypocrisy (Matthew 23:13–33; Luke 12:1).
- Self-righteousness (Luke 16:15).
- False teaching (Matthew 23:2–8; Matthew 16:6–12).
- Self-importance (Luke 20:46–47).

His criticisms weren't nice, polite discussions,

either. Although He could be gentle and tender with those who repented of sin, with the stiff-necked religious leaders Jesus was forthright to the point of insult:

"They devour widows' houses and for a show make lengthy prayers. Such men will be punished most severely" (Luke 20:47).

"They tie up heavy loads and put them on men's shoulders, but they themselves are not willing to lift a finger to move them" (Matthew 23:4).

"Everything they do is done for men to see" (Matthew 23:5).

"You belong to your father, the devil, and you want to carry out your father's desire. He was a murderer from the beginning, not holding to the truth, for there is no truth in him. When he lies, he speaks his native language, for he is a liar and the father of lies" (John 8:44).

With words like these piercing their self-righteousness, no wonder the Pharisees and Sadducees weren't praising Jesus. They didn't want to lose their authority over the people, and they didn't want others to know of their wrongdoing.

> **According to Josephus, there were only about 6,000 Pharisees in Jesus' day. These Pharisees were not necessarily scholars, although there were rabbis among them (Acts 5:34).[25]**

So it's not surprising that the Babylonian Talmud, a collection of Jewish rabbinical laws and opinions, refers to Jesus as a sorcerer.[26] Though the Babylonian Talmud was compiled about 500 years after Jesus' death and resurrection, the information for it would have come from Jesus' enemies.

Though the names may have changed, today some people still attack Jesus, claiming He wanted to put one over on others. But how many con men or sorcerers have followers centuries later—followers who would die for them? After allowing for his errors, one might follow an honest man who was honestly mistaken in some of his beliefs. But how would a real con man get so many followers over the centuries without being found out?

A thoroughly investigated man like Jesus *would* eventually be found out and uncovered. There are testimonies concerning Him. People who knew Him and His ministry were alive when His story was told. Through the centuries the evidence has been pored over. Yet many who started out as doubters have found themselves believing that Jesus is who He claimed to be once they critically considered the evidence.

The Claims of Jesus

If Jesus were planning on being a con man, He certainly didn't go about it in the ordinary way. He didn't use smooth lines to convince others but straightforward speeches and confrontations with the religious hierarchy of His day. He made no efforts to make His followers happy by telling them what they wanted to hear, but instead He talked of taking up a cross and giving up wrongdoing.

Even more amazing are the claims Jesus makes for Himself and the way He speaks of God. . . . Why it was enough to shock any faithful Jew!

> Naturally God's message produces a remarkable response in the hearers. . . . This has led some to conclude that the Bible's inspiration lies in its impact on them—on the fact that it inspires them. But they are wrong. . . . The fact of its inspiration in no way depends on its being received by men.[27]

A Father-Son Relationship

The Old Testament speaks of God as a Father (Deuteronomy 1:31), but when Jesus spoke of God as His Father, the Jewish leaders could tell He was talking about something different from the distant paternal relationship they found acceptable. Jesus' words expressed an unusually close relationship with God. The Gospel writer John reports that Jesus frequently said He did His Father's will (John 5:19–20; 6:39–40, 57; 7:16–19; 8:28–29; 9:4; 12:49–50). Indeed, Jesus uses this claim to support His actions and His authority to do them.

For us, such complete obedience to a parent would seem unusual. Who among us can say we do our parents' will with anything approaching such intensity? Still, few would fault Jesus for that.

But there was more to Jesus' claim than that. The religious leaders got Jesus' key point one day when they attacked Him for healing on the Sabbath. Jesus replied, "My Father is always at his work to this very day, and I, too, am working." John explains the connection the leaders immediately made and their reaction to it: "For this reason the Jews tried all the harder to kill him; not only was he breaking the Sabbath, but he was even calling God his own Father, making himself equal with God" (John 5:17–18). Already the leaders had been looking for a way to get rid of a man who threatened their authority, but now their need for action became more intense.

Jesus' claim to a close relationship with the Father would have been doubly offensive to religious Jews because as far as they were concerned, Jesus was illegitimate—hadn't His mother suddenly become pregnant, and she not yet married? This is the man who claims God as Father? they would have thought. Closeness to God would have been the last thing they would have imagined Jesus to have. More likely, to their minds, was that He should be an outcast, just as His mother should have been.

As Jesus claimed God as His Father, He wasn't only claiming an unusually intimate God-to-human spiritual relationship. Though today's readers of the Scriptures may miss the point, the Jews did not. They knew Psalm 2:7–9, 12:

> I will proclaim the decree of the Lord:
> He said to me, "You are my Son; today I
> have become your Father. Ask of me, and I
> will make the nations your inheritance, the
> ends of the earth your possession. You will
> rule them with an iron scepter; you will
> dash them to pieces like pottery. . . . Kiss
> the Son, lest he be angry and you be
> destroyed in your way.

The Jews recognized that Jesus was referring to this messianic prophecy. For years the Jews had looked for their Messiah, whom they expected to save political Israel. He would be a powerful figure chosen by God for his service.

But just in case they missed His claim, Jesus went beyond Sonship and claimed equality with God by saying that what God did—working on the day of rest—He also did. The Jews rested on the Sabbath because God had rested after creation and in the Ten Commandments had declared the day holy. Trying to escape the law's requirement to rest on the Sabbath was blasphemy because it denied the commandment; the biblical punishment for breaking the commandment was death.

Unless, of course, Jesus really was the Messiah.

An Unusual Son

Perhaps critics may try to maintain that those leaders misunderstood Jesus (though it would seem hard to do that in light of the verses that follow that passage). But even if the leaders did misunderstand, other Scriptures recording Jesus' words still present a challenge to those who want to discount His testimony. Consider some of the claims this Son made for Himself:

- He came from the Father (John 8:42; John 16:27–28).
- The Son brings glory to the Father (John 14:13).

- He who knows the Son knows the Father
  (Matthew 11:27; John 8:19; John 14:7).
- He who welcomes the Son welcomes the
  Father (Luke 9:48).
- He who honors the Son honors the Father
  (John 5:23).
- He who sees the Son sees the Father
  (John 14:9–11).
- He who receives a believer in Me receives Me
  and My Father (Matthew 10:40).
- The Father gives life and judgment to the Son
  (John 5:21–22).
- The Father gives the Son His seal of approval
  (John 6:27).
- The Father witnesses to the ministry of the Son
  (John 8:18).
- The Father will answer prayer in the Son's
  name (Matthew 18:19–20; John 14:14;
  John 16:23–24).

Though clearly Jesus was not thinking about His relationship with His earthly father, Joseph, some of these claims might be part of an unusually close father-son relationship. A friend of a father might welcome his son, because of that friendship. But few of us, no matter how devoted we are, would claim that God would answer prayers in our names. And in Jesus' day, that idea would have been foreign. Nowhere in the Old Testament Scriptures is one person instructed to pray in the name of another. No one in Jesus' day would have claimed to have a special connection to God that would go straight to the Father's heart.

It would be hard to imagine that someone who claims all this would not come off sounding at least incredibly self-important, bordering on mentally unstable. Even Jesus' closest friends could hardly have ignored that, especially where the Father concerned was God. Yet even Jesus' enemies never leveled that charge at Him.

As little as they liked it, the Jewish leaders had gotten it right. The relationship between Jesus and the Father was not your normal father-son relationship or even an average spiritual relationship. Jesus claimed something extraordinary for Himself: a special relationship with God. Add to that Jesus' declaration that He was Lord of the Sabbath (Matthew 12:8; Mark 2:27–28; and Luke 6:3–5), and it's clear Jesus was doing more than simply pointing out that the Jews had made too many petty rules about the day of rest.

More Than a Son

Jesus often spoke of His relationship with God the Father, but even a close human son would hesitate to speak for His father as Jesus did. Throughout the Gospels, Jesus constantly interpreted God the Father for His followers. His interpretations of the law surprised listeners, who commented, "he taught as one who had authority, and not as their teachers of the law" (Matthew 7:29). Jesus went way beyond the religious leaders in His understanding of what God was like and what He expected of His people.

At this point we might be tempted to see Jesus as an extraordinary prophet. But even a prophet might hesitate to make some of these claims or interpretations:

- Fasting should be done in secret (Matthew 6:16–18).
- God does not want His children to be lost (Matthew 18:14).

- God knows and provides for every need
  (Luke 12:30–31; Matthew 6:30;
  Matthew 6:8).
- God has given the disciples His kingdom
  (Luke 12:32).
- God will bring justice for His people who pray
  (Luke 18:6).
- To be part of God's kingdom takes childlike
  faith (Mark 10:14–15; Luke 18:16–17).
- Those who suffer for the Son will have eternal
  life (Matthew 19:29–30).
- In heaven people will not marry (Matthew
  22:29–32; Luke 20:34–38).
- Moses allowed divorce because people were
  hardhearted, but it was not God's desire
  (Matthew 19:8–9).
- A time would come when the earth
  would end (Matthew 24:35–41;
  Mark 13:31–34).
- Anyone who did not think His [Jesus'] words
  were from God would not be forgiven
  (Mark 3:28–30).
- Anyone accepting the Son is accepted by the
  Father (John 14:20; John 17:21).

Jesus spoke for God and made amazing claims about Him and His own relationship with God. Even very devoted followers, people who might speak *about* God, would hesitate to speak *for* Him. No wonder the religious leaders of Jesus' day had a problem with His statements. How could someone really know what God thought on a subject? Jesus had to be a sorcerer or a con man, the religious leaders decided. These were the only logical possibilities!

More Outrageous Claims

Surely anyone who made all these claims must have been standing on the edge of insanity. Normal people do not make such demands of our belief systems. When they do, it isn't long before we get them medical and psychiatric help. We don't usually see such individuals leading large groups of disciples, though a few madmen may gather a small band.

Had Jesus' claims ended here, we could easily discount Him. But that is not where it ends. Jesus makes even more claims. Though the terminology He uses may be unfamiliar to us, if we understand something of the world He came into, we can begin to see the magnitude of what He was claiming.

Messiah

Today we may not be familiar with this word. Many more people know it as the word *Christ*. But even then, we're muddy about what it means.

To first-century Jews, the Messiah would be a powerful man sent by God to save his people. Often they thought of him as a military man who would remove their country from the grasp of Rome. Roman oppression had pushed to the front the thought that this savior would be someone who could make their country free and great.

But the theme of the Messiah is broader than that. From the Old Testament prophecies, the Jews recognized that the Messiah would also be greater than any of their prophets (Deuteronomy 18:18) and a wise king (Psalm 2:6). In the first century, however, the popular concept of the Messiah ignored the suffering servant described in Isaiah 53. When Jesus came as the suffering one, He didn't fit the picture the priests and elders expected.

> He was despised and rejected by men,
> a man of sorrows, and familiar with
> suffering. . . .
> Surely he took up our infirmities and
> carried our sorrows, yet we considered him
> stricken by God. . . .
> But he was pierced for our transgressions. . .
> and by his wounds we are healed. . . .
> And the LORD has laid on him the iniquity
> of us all. ISAIAH 53:3–6

Messiah means "anointed one," and *Christ* comes from the Greek word for "anointing." Usually kings were anointed to establish their divine right to rule. The Messiah or Christ would be one chosen by God to rule the earth.

Son of God

The messianic king is also God's Son (Psalm 2:6–9). When the chief priests and council of elders asked Jesus if He was the Christ (they would have said "Messiah," but Luke was reporting to a Greek-speaking world, so he used the Greek term), Jesus called Himself the Son of Man (Luke 22:69). This was a term Jesus often used to describe Himself, one that emphasized His humanity. The leaders knew He had said nothing wrong and wanted to force Him into words that were clearly blasphemous, so they pressed the question, asking, "Are you then the Son of God?"

"You are right in saying I am," He replied (verse 70).

In John 5, Jesus makes some amazing claims concerning His relationship with the Father that can be better understood in the context of verses 25–27, where Jesus said:

> I tell you the truth, a time is coming and has now come when the dead will hear the voice of the Son of God and those who hear will live. For as the Father has life in himself, so he has granted the Son to have life in

himself. And he has given him authority to judge because he is the Son of Man.

Clearly, Jesus was speaking of Himself. He was connecting the Son of God and the Son of Man. Jews would have known the verses in Daniel's prophecy (7:13–14):

> Before me was one like a son of man, coming with the clouds of heaven. He approached the Ancient of Days [God] and was led into his presence. He was given authority, glory and sovereign power; all peoples, nations, and men of every language worshiped him. His dominion is an everlasting dominion that will not pass away, and his kingdom is one that will never be destroyed.

John 9 reports that after Jesus healed the blind man and the Jewish leaders had thrown the man out, Jesus sought the man out and asked, "Do you believe in the Son of Man?" When Jesus identified Himself as the Son of Man, the man worshiped

Him. Obviously, the man had made the connection between those verses and Jesus' question.

Who Is This Man?

Now, any sane and humble man, finding someone worshiping Him, would set the record straight. When Paul and Barnabas were called gods by the people of Lystra, Paul wasted no time in correcting them (Acts 14:11–15). But Jesus did not stop the man from worshiping or declare at any time that He was not Messiah. He did not correct Peter, when Peter called Him Christ (Matthew 16:16); instead, Jesus commended him (verse 17). However, He did not command His followers to spread the news; in verse 20, He asked them not to tell anyone.

Speaking to the woman at the well, He identified Himself as the Christ (John 4:26). When she spread the news to her village, the people said, "We know that this man really is the Savior of the world" (John 4:42).

Although Jesus never made a flat statement to the crowds, "I am the Messiah," we cannot doubt that this was His message. Confrontation with the

Jewish leaders would come soon enough; in failing to make a blunt statement, He was not retracting His claims. He simply spoke wisely, to people receptive to the truth.

Is Jesus God?

Many who read the New Testament say Jesus never claimed to be God. He may not have declared, "I am God" in those words, but that does not mean He did not say it.

"Your father Abraham rejoiced at the thought of seeing my day; he saw it and was glad," Jesus told the Jewish leaders who opposed Him. Naturally they were confused at that and pointed out that He was not even fifty years old. How could He claim to have seen Abraham, who lived thousands of years before?

" 'I tell you the truth,' Jesus answered, 'before Abraham was born, I am!' " (John 8:56–58). At this, the Jews picked up stones to stone Him for blasphemy. They knew He was referring to Exodus 3:14, when Moses asked God what His name was, and

"God said to Moses, 'I AM WHO I AM. This is what you are to say to the Israelites: "I AM has sent me to you." ' " Jesus *was* claiming to be God.

> The sayings of Jesus alone contain over 40 actual quotations from the Old Testament, the letters of Paul nearly 100, and the total for the New Testament as a whole is something like 250. . . . The New Testament writers were so steeped in the Old Testament that its language came naturally to them.[28]

Shortly after that, Jesus said, "I and the Father are one." Again the Jews tried to stone Him. When He asked what miracles He had done to merit such punishment, they replied, "We are not stoning you for any of these. . .but for blasphemy, because you, a mere man, claim to be God" (John 10:30–33).

Was Jesus Wicked?

Jesus clearly made huge claims for Himself. If we listen to C. S. Lewis's advice, we need to consider whether He was a lunatic or a devil. But the man presented in Scripture is clearheaded and rational, not a lunatic. If the apostles had been lying about that, surely the evidence would have come forth through the Pharisees and Sadducees. And what of Jesus' miracles? All it would have taken to disprove them was one person to say the miracle hadn't lasted, that it had been only a trick. But never, through a three-year ministry, does someone come forward to make this claim. Jesus' enemies would not have hesitated to bring forth any news that was not to His credit. They also had the ability to pass around the information, so it wouldn't have been a secret for long. But we hear not even a rumor of such a thing.

So that leaves us with the second possibility: that Jesus was truly wicked. To believe this, one would have to discount all the testimony of the Gospels. Could Jesus have so confused twelve men, perhaps not all well-educated but nevertheless men who were well accustomed to the rough and tumble of the first-century world? Could He really have convinced them all that He was incredibly good had He actually been incredibly wicked?

> If Jesus was a liar, a con man, and therefore an evil, foolish man, then how can we explain the fact that He left us the most profound moral instruction and powerful moral example that anyone ever has left?[29]

To believe that Jesus was wicked, one would have to also believe that all twelve of His disciples were fairly naïve or wicked themselves. But even if the original eleven were, what about Paul? Paul *was* an educated man. Why would he, the chief persecutor of Christians after the Crucifixion, suddenly change sides? He had no reason to change his affiliation. Yet Acts 9 reports an astonishing supernatural challenge on the road to Damascus and a subsequent healing. The one who reports these events is the physician Luke— another well-educated man who would be unlikely to naïvely accept any false report.

Jesus was neither a lunatic nor a devil. The Gospel testimony, taken on its own merits, does not report on any such man.

But there's still another testimony in His favor— one that was written before He came to earth.

4

THE LAW AND THE PROPHETS ON JESUS

What does the Old Testament say about Jesus' claims?

If Jesus wasn't a lunatic or wicked, He *must* have been a fraud. After all, people just don't do these things! It couldn't have happened that way.

Many have tried to claim that Jesus' acts and claims were all the work of a smooth con man. But just as the other cases against Him are not easy to make, this one has some real problems. In the last chapter, a few of these problems were mentioned.

But, to make their case, the fraud seekers must also accept the unlikely idea that none of the disciples or apostles would have let the cat out of the bag. The apostles, highly moral men who willingly gave their lives for the message they proclaimed, surely would have had among them one who would have felt guilty and divulged the plot. Or if they too were con men, surely one of them would have sought to escape the life-threatening consequences of adherence to Christian beliefs by denouncing the plot.

But a still more powerful testimony must be discredited to accept the fraud theory: the Old Testament prophecies. Though the count may vary slightly, according to Josh McDowell, Jesus fulfilled over three hundred Old Testament prophecies[30]— including some that were not even recognized as messianic prophecies until after He fulfilled them.

One might imagine that an elaborate plot existed to make Jesus the Messiah. But if that were true, what gain would come to Jesus or His apostles? Death and persecution for the apostles and a life in hiding for a "risen" Jesus? It hardly seems worth the effort it would have taken to manage to fulfill so many prophecies—to say nothing of the problem of covering up the conflicting prophecies over which these men would have had no control!

Imagine the unlikely chance of getting people to agree so fully and so flawlessly to go along with such an elaborate fraud! In order to fulfill the Old Testament prophecies, the plot would have to include as "conspirators" some Jews who lived centuries before the fraud, Jesus' parents, and others who were part of the renegade Jewish sect that became Christianity.

When the first [Bible] manuscripts were copied they weren't done in some cavalier, haphazard fashion. The Jewish copyists took their work seriously: the discovery of even the smallest error could lead to the whole manuscript being destroyed and work beginning all over again.[31]

The Old Testament Message[32]

Okay, so maybe it was all coincidence, you may be saying about now. *Maybe Jesus just* happened *to fulfill the prophecies.*

The Old Testament, written over a one-thousand-year period, contains nearly three hundred references to the coming Messiah.[33]

I'm afraid that sheer coincidence is not likely at all. The chance of just eight—not to mention roughly three hundred—prophecies being fulfilled is 1 in 100 million billion. That's the same chance as if you covered the state of Texas with silver dollars to the depth of two feet, blindfolded someone, and asked that person to pick up on the first try a single marked dollar that was somewhere among them.[34]

In looking for messianic references, understand that no single Old Testament passage outlines everything about the Messiah. Instead the messianic theme runs through the various books of Scripture. There's no clear "messianic checklist" in Scripture. But we don't need to deal with the entire set of prophecies here. We just need eight that Jesus or His followers would not have been able to control to show that Jesus had to be who He claimed to be.

His Birth

People can control a lot of things, but they can't control to whom they were born. The Old Testament prophecies give a very specific lineage for the Messiah, one that stemmed from the line of David. "When your days are over and you rest with your fathers," the prophet Nathan told David, speaking for God, "I will raise up your offspring to succeed you, who will come from your own body, and I will establish his kingdom. . . . I will establish the throne of his kingdom forever" (2 Samuel 7:12–13). Jeremiah 23:5 applies this promise to the Messiah, who will come from David's line. In the New Testament, Luke 1:27 identifies Mary as being from the line of David. If you trace Jesus' lineage back, with the other prophecies that define other parts of the Messiah's ancestry, Jesus has the right birth line.

Nor can one control one's place of birth. Asked by Herod where the king of the Jews would be born, the chief priests and teachers of the law had no trouble identifying the spot. They quoted Micah 5:2 (Matthew 2:3–6). But though many Old Testament scholars would have known that the Messiah would be born in Bethlehem, and skeptics might think Mary and Joseph engineered the place of their son's birth, the two Jewish peasants could never have engineered a Roman census, decreed by the distant emperor. Through a pagan emperor's act, Jesus was born not in the family home in Nazareth but in Bethlehem.

Jeremiah 31:15 prophesies the killing of children, causing Rachel (who stands as a symbol of Israel) to weep. Matthew 2:16–18 connects the historical incident of Herod's slaying of Bethlehem's infants with Jeremiah's prophecy. There is no way anyone could have planned such an event—certainly Herod would never have intentionally done anything that would have proved Jesus Messiah.

These three prophecies are fulfilled while Jesus is just an infant, unable to make up a plot or control anything about His life.

His Death and Crucifixion

In Jesus' death and crucifixion, many prophecies are fulfilled in a short time. Consider the following ones that neither Jesus nor His followers would have had an opportunity to manipulate in any way.

His Betrayal

Matthew 27:3 reports that the price Judas received from the chief priests and elders was thirty pieces of silver. His enemies decided on the price—and in doing so missed the fact that they were fulfilling Zechariah 11:12–13:

> I told them, "If you think it best, give me my pay; but if not, keep it." So they paid me thirty pieces of silver. And the LORD said to me, "Throw it to the potter"—the handsome price at which they priced me! So I took the thirty pieces of silver and threw them into the house of the LORD to the potter.

The facetious "handsome price" was the price of a slave in Zechariah's day. But the priests and elders obviously did not connect these verses with a prophecy fulfilled, or they would never have given

Judas that amount—one piece more or less, and no one would have seen this as a messianic prophecy. Surely Jesus' enemies would never have wanted to do anything that might help out His case.

Judas fulfilled another prophecy when he went to the Jews and tossed their blood money into the temple (Matthew 27:3–5). Since some might claim that he was somehow set up by Jesus and His disciples, we will not include this in our eight. But it's unlikely that the one who turned against Jesus and then hanged himself in remorse would have intentionally made such a mistake.

"Throw it to the potter" was a second prophecy unintentionally fulfilled by the priests and elders when they "decided to use the money to buy the potter's field as a burial place for foreigners." Matthew comments, "That is why it has been called the Field of Blood to this day" (Matthew 27:6–8).

The Crucifixion

After Jesus' arrest many prophecies are fulfilled. A large number, concerning the Crucifixion, are included in Psalm 22, which we'll cover later. But let's look first at the abuse meted out to Jesus before the cross. The Old Testament prophecies are fulfilled in the New Testament passages below.

Incident	Old Testament Prophecy
He was hit in the face	Micah 5:1
He was spit upon	Isaiah 50:6
He was mocked	Isaiah 50:6
He was scourged	Isaiah 50:6

New Testament Fulfillment

John 18:22; John 19:3

Matthew 27:30; Mark 14:65

Matthew 27:29; Mark 15:17–18; Luke 22:63–65; John 19:2–3

Matthew 27:26; Mark 15:15; John 19:1

Jesus or His followers could not have controlled any of these actions.

Crucifixion was a purely Roman method of death. Had Jesus been put to death for blasphemy according to the Jewish law, He would have been stoned. But under the laws of the Roman Empire, the Jews had no authority to kill, which is why the Jewish leaders who wanted to end His life had to involve Rome in their dispute with Jesus.

> **Archeological support is not available for every Biblical event. Yet it is true to say that it has corroborated the substantial historicity of the Biblical record from the patriarchal age to the apostolic age.**[35]

Crucifixion was an incredibly painful form of death intended for the worst criminals. It was the Jews, not the Roman authorities, who insisted that Jesus be crucified (John 18:31–32; 19:6). The Jewish leaders were saying that Jesus was a terrible criminal. Yet despite the exquisite suffering that crucifixion inflicted and the presumed guilt of the one who experienced it, God upheld Jesus' righteousness by not allowing His bones to be broken (Psalm 34:19–20; John 19:33). The psalm was both a prophecy and a vindication of Jesus.

Instead of breaking Jesus' legs—the common practice to hurry the end of a crucifixion—when the

Roman soldiers came to Jesus, seeing that He was already dead, they pierced His side with a spear (John 19:33–34). As they did so, they fulfilled the prophetic words of Zechariah 12:10: "They will look on me, the one they have pierced."

Already we have more than eight prophecies fulfilled in Jesus—prophecies the disciples could not have faked. But there is still another psalm, written centuries before the Crucifixion, that bears an uncanny resemblance to the events of that day.

Psalm 22

On the cross, Jesus cried out, "My God, my God, why have you forsaken me?" but that first verse of Psalm 22 is not the only verse that describes the Crucifixion. The psalm is heavily loaded with messianic prophecy, fulfilled in the hours of Jesus' death.

Prophecy	Psalm 22
Scorned and despised	6–7
He trusted in God, let God save him	8
All my bones are out of joint	14
They pierced my hands and feet	16
They divide my garments among them and cast lots for my clothing	18

New Testament Fulfillment

Matthew 27:37–44

Matthew 27:43; Luke 23:35

Crucifixion would have dislocated his arms.[36]

Crucifixion included nails being driven through the hands and feet

Matthew 27:35; Luke 23:34; John 19:23–24

One of the most amazing things about Psalm 22 is that all these descriptions accurately describe a Roman crucifixion that would occur centuries later.

Discovering eight prophecies fulfilled by Jesus is no problem—in fact there are many more.[37] But here are a few clear evidences that any skeptic needs to consider. Based on the Old Testament evidence, it is fair to say that Jesus really was just who He said He was. No other man could have filled the bill so clearly described by men who lived hundreds of years before Jesus set foot on earth.

You could say that you just picked up that single marked silver dollar. And those dollars spread all over Texas add up to more than the number of people who have lived in this world, down through the ages.[38]

It's not rocket science to figure that Jesus is who He said He was!

5

WHAT THE EARLY CHURCH SAID ABOUT JESUS

**A look into what the early
church said about Jesus,
through the Book of Acts
and the early confessions.**

Everything we've looked at about Jesus pales in comparison to any consideration of His last days on earth and the events that followed them. The most amazing things are yet to come, though He only spoke beforehand of them. For the death and resurrection of Jesus, we must again rely on the apostles' message.

Before His Death

Jesus repeatedly predicted His own death and resurrection. He knew the mission God had sent Him on, and He tried to warn the disciples of coming events. As so often happens, these totally foreign ideas fell on deaf ears. Not until after the fact did the eleven disciples who would spread Jesus' message to the world begin to understand their Master's words.

Jesus foretold His own death and resurrection when He visited the Temple and cleared it of the moneychangers, who extorted money from those who wanted to offer a sacrifice to God. When His angry opponents asked for a sign that He had the authority to do such a thing, Jesus told them, "Destroy this temple, and I will raise it again in three days" (John 2:19). The confused Jews pointed out that it had taken forty-six years to build the Temple. How would Jesus rebuild it in three days? Not until after His death, did the disciples understand that in speaking of the temple, Jesus had been referring to His body, not the place of worship in Jerusalem (verse 22).

In Matthew 12:40, Jesus again referred to His resurrection when He compared Himself to Jonah, who spent three days in the belly of the fish. The Pharisees and teachers of the law remembered this statement after His death, when they asked the Romans to guard Jesus' tomb.

Despite the fact that the disciples had Jesus to explain things to them, they did not understand many of the prophecies their Master made referring to His death and resurrection. Jesus told them, "In a little while you will see me no more, and then after a little while you will see me," and the disciples wondered what He meant (John 16:16–18). Jesus understood their confusion; He promised that someday He would speak plainly and they would understand (verse 25).

Once, when Jesus tried to talk about His death, Peter began to take Him to task (Mark 8:31–32). As close as he was to Jesus, Peter still was not ready for the events that were to take place. But Jesus did not force the information on His disciples. He knew they would have the Old Testament prophecies, along with the Holy Spirit, to help them understand His death (John 16:12–15). In His post-Resurrection appearances, Jesus would explain the Old Testament prophecies to His followers (Luke 24:25–27, 45–47).

In the space of some seventy years after their leader had been crucified for alleged blasphemy and treason, Christians had reached every corner of the Empire and were circulating documents about the life of Jesus and letters of encouragement and instruction from the apostles.[39]

The Resurrection Accounts

All four Gospel writers provide accounts of Jesus' death and resurrection (Matthew 27–28; Mark 15–16; Luke 22–24; John 19–20). Indeed these events are the most important of His ministry—this was the reason why Jesus came to earth.

With minor differences, which are probably caused by the testimonies of different witnesses to the events, the Gospel writers tell the same story.[40] The women went to the tomb where Jesus had been hastily laid on the night before the Sabbath. His body was missing. There the women saw the stone rolled away from the tomb and Jesus gone. An angel told them He was risen, as He had said He would be. The women ran for the other disciples, and John and

Peter came to check out what happened. They too saw that Jesus was gone, and they noted that the grave clothes could not have been unwrapped.

With these multiple and independent accounts [of the Resurrection] no historian would disregard this evidence [the Gospels] just because of secondary discrepancies.[41]

The Resurrection is *the* point of Christianity. Without it, Christianity *would* simply be a hoax. The Resurrection is the single event around which the New Testament revolves. The early church affirmed this remarkable event, despite persecution; and the fearful disciples, once filled with the promised Spirit, brought news of the Resurrection to the Roman world.

Our Lord has written the promise of the resurrection not in books alone, but in every leaf in springtime.
Martin Luther

Considering the reliability of the Scriptures, their careful documentation of the events surrounding the death and resurrection of Jesus, and the actions of the early church, we cannot discount the Resurrection. Jesus was seen alive after His death and not by just a few people. He appeared to ten of His disciples just after His Resurrection (John 20:19–20). He appeared to Thomas, who had not been with the others, a week later (John 20:24–29). Then He appeared to seven of the disciples while they were fishing (John 21). He appeared to two disciples on the road to Emmaus (Luke 24:13–35), who mentioned that He had previously appeared to Peter (verse 34). He appeared to the disciples in Galilee (Matthew 28:16) and again near Bethany at His ascension (Luke 24:50–51).

Paul, who was not part of the Christian community at this point, later reported that Jesus "appeared to more than five hundred of the brothers at the same time, most of whom are still living" (1 Corinthians 15:6). There were plenty of people to testify to the Resurrection, having all seen Jesus at various times. Their testimony was enough to convince the scholarly Paul, though he had not been among them.

The Jews' Case

On top of the testimonies for the Resurrection, the Jews who opposed Jesus made no credible argument against it. They had insisted the Romans put a guard on the tomb, and Pilate had obliged them. But when the guards came to the chief priests to explain what had happened, the spiritual leaders of Israel bribed them. Matthew reports they told the guards, "You are to say, 'His disciples came during the night and stole him away while we were asleep.' If this report gets to the governor, we will satisfy him and keep you out of trouble" (Matthew 27:64–66; 28:11–14). The guard would not have been in a rush to tell their leaders anything, since sleeping on guard duty could have cost them their lives.[42] To say the least, the Roman military took a dim view of such incompetence. If the priests got them out of their difficulty, the guards would have been happy to go along with the plan and keep their mouths shut. What did it matter to them if the Jews were having a religious problem?

Strange, isn't it, that the Jews didn't push the Roman rulers to search out the body of Jesus? Nor did they look into the facts themselves. The disciples were still in Jerusalem, easy enough for a determined soldier or Jewish leader to find. But even though the religious rulers claimed Jesus' body was stolen, they did nothing to prove this was so. Doubtless the Gospel writers would have included the story of such a search in their account, since this would have increased their own danger at a time when they were already frightened. Instead, Matthew reports that the story the Jews gave to the guards was widely circulated at the time he was writing (Matthew 28:15). A strangely pat answer for a disturbing situation, isn't it?

What Christians Believe

In one of his letters, Paul provides us with an outline of what Christians believe about the death and resurrection of Jesus:

> Now, brothers, I want to remind you of the gospel I preached to you, which you received and on which you have taken your stand. By this gospel you are saved, if you hold firmly to the word I preached to you.

Otherwise, you have believed in vain. For what I received I passed on to you as of first importance: that Christ died for our sins according to the Scriptures, that he was buried, that he was raised on the third day according to the Scriptures, and that he appeared to Peter, and then to the Twelve (1 Corinthians 15:1–5).

From this passage, we can see that Paul saw these things as being the core of Christian teaching:

- Christ died for our sins, following the prophecies of Scripture.
- Christ was buried.
- Christ was raised on the third day (again following Scripture).

Jesus' death and resurrection, the key points of Christianity, are testified to by both the Old Testament prophets and the numerous first-century eyewitnesses. Paul passed this message on to the early church. Indeed, he says that this gospel will save those to whom he preaches. The apostle's teaching wasn't a take-it-or-leave-it affair. Either you believed and were a Christian—or you didn't believe and you weren't.

Christianity begins where religion ends...with the Resurrection.

Anonymous

Paul simply identified the issues we need to take seriously. Though Christian denominations have split over other, less serious questions, those need not concern us here. We want to consider the core message that makes Christianity Christian. All Christian denominations share these three beliefs. To deny them is to become something other than Christian.

But these three simple ideas are loaded with meaning. They contain a number of more serious implications.

Christ died for our sins

These few simple words imply much more than we might expect. Consider the ideas implicit here.

- Jesus really did die.
- There is such a thing as sin.

- Jesus did not die for His own sins (because He was sinless).
- We sinned.
- We needed someone to die for us.

Paul takes sin seriously. He describes what later theologians would call "substitutionary atonement." The basic truth conveyed by this phrase is that we were sinful and Jesus died in our place, as a sacrifice for sin, so that we, like Him, could be raised to new life. Because we were sinful, we could not have a relationship with a holy God who cannot tolerate sin. To enable us to have a relationship, someone had to pay the price for that sin. Jesus paid it by sacrificing His sinless life, because only a blood sacrifice could cover sin (Genesis 3:21). Through Jesus' sacrifice, God's justice was satisfied, so that He could give forgiveness and not ignore the wrong that was done.

What is sin?
Sin is any want of conformity unto, or transgression of, the law of God.

The Shorter Catechism

Today you won't find *sin* a big topic of discussion in most circles. But it wasn't always that way. In Paul's day, Jews believed that any wrongdoing they'd committed required the death of an animal, a sacrifice to God that took the place of the sinner, so that God could forgive that wrongdoing. The animal was a substitute that died for the sin, in place of the sinner—it was a symbolic substitutionary atonement. This was the Old Testament law that God had established centuries before Jesus came to earth.

For Christians, that Old Testament sacrifice is a symbol of the sacrifice of Christ on the cross. The Old Testament faithful were looking forward to the day when the Messiah would come and be the substitute for their sins. Christians believe that Jesus, the Messiah, is that perfect sacrifice. Because He was the sinless Son of God, He did not have any sins to be forgiven, so when we believe in Him, His death brings us forgiveness.

Why does the Creed say, "I believe in the forgiveness of sins"?

I believe in the forgiveness of sins because through Christ, God has declared pardon and forgiveness to all sinful humanity.[43]

In Paul's writing, he points out that Jesus' death followed the scriptural prophecies. By this he is saying that Jesus is Messiah, just who He said He was. Paul was an up-and-coming Pharisee at the time of his conversion. He knew the messianic Scriptures we've already considered, and he is reminding his readers that Jesus fulfilled them.

Christ was buried

When Paul affirms this second point, he is establishing the reality of Jesus' death. Not only was Jesus' death real, He spent time in a tomb. The claims that His body was removed from the tomb by His followers are not true. Paul testifies that the Crucifixion was a real death. Without it, the sacrifice we just discussed would be meaningless. We would all still be bound by our sins.

Christ was raised on the third day

Normally, people don't die and reappear alive to hundreds of people. No one else who has ever lived on earth has been able to make this claim with any validity. Again, Paul is testifying to Jesus' divinity. Another way Paul supports this point is by reminding his readers of the prophecies fulfilled (Psalm 16:8–11; 30:3; John 2:19; Matthew 12:40).

Jesus was also raised just at the right time. Though many nowadays question this, since three full days did not pass before His resurrection, according to the way that the Jews of that era counted time, a part of a day was referred to as a full day. So Jesus died on Friday, lay in the grave all day Saturday, and rose early on the third day.

You might say that Paul is reminding his readers that Jesus really is God. They have placed their trust in Him, and that is what will save them for eternity. Because Jesus died and was raised again, those who believe He is the Son of God, sent to die for their sin, will be reconciled with God.

What moves God to forgive sins?
God forgives sins because He is merciful and because of Christ's atoning sacrifice for sinners.⁴⁴

Perhaps a friend—or even someone on the street— has asked if you are "saved." That's another word that doesn't have much meaning for most people nowadays—unless they are drowning. It's a word Paul used fairly often, though, in his writings. His full meaning comes through when you read Romans 5:9–11:

> Since we have now been justified by his blood, how much more shall we be saved from God's wrath through him! For if, when we were God's enemies, we were reconciled to him through the death of his Son, how much more, having been reconciled, shall we be saved through his life! Not only is this so, but we also rejoice in God through our Lord Jesus Christ, through whom we have now received reconciliation.

Being "saved" is all about reconciliation with God—we are saved from His wrath and have peace with Him. That's why Jesus' sacrifice on the cross and His resurrection three days later are important. Because He was raised from the dead, after sacrificing Himself for our sins, we too can have new life. All we must do is believe that He died for our sin and turn from that sin.

The mystery of the humanity of Christ, that He sunk Himself into our flesh, is beyond all human understanding.

Martin Luther

Early Church Beliefs

After the death of the apostles, the same ideas Paul outlined were taught to Christians. They are still with us today, in fact, through the early church creeds.

The Apostles' Creed and the Early Church

The earliest of the Christian creeds that was passed on to the church is the Apostles' Creed. This creed from the first or second century A.D. closely follows the teachings of Scripture. You might say that it's simply a rewriting of the most basic scriptural truths into a concise form.

I believe in God the Father, Almighty,

Maker of heaven and earth; and in Jesus
Christ, his only begotten Son, our Lord;
who was conceived by the Holy Ghost, born
of the Virgin Mary; suffered under Pontius
Pilate; was crucified, dead and buried; He
descended into hell; the third day he rose
again from the dead; He ascended into
heaven, and sits at the right hand of God
the Father Almighty; from thence he shall
come to judge the quick and the dead; I
believe in the Holy Ghost; I believe in the
holy catholic church; the communion of
saints; the forgiveness of sins; the resurrection of the body; and the life everlasting.
Amen.

Note that the elements in Paul's simple three-
point creed are all here: Jesus died, was buried, and
was raised. The other elements are all from Scripture
as well.

The Apostles' Creed sums up in a few words the
main points of our redemption, and thus may serve as a

tablet for us upon which we see distinctly and point by
point the things in Christ that we ought to heed.

John Calvin

Polycarp

Another testimony to early Christian beliefs was
written by Polycarp. This bishop of Smyrna was what
you might call a second-generation Christian. He
was born sometime around A.D. 65–69, and he knew
the apostles.

By this time some heresies had begun to creep
into the church. The apostles fought them, but erro-
neous ideas about Christ and His message continued.
People who had ideas that were different from what
the apostles taught infiltrated the church, so Polycarp
returned believers to the basic beliefs that make
Christianity what it is. He preached:

"For whosoever does not confess that
Jesus Christ has come in the flesh, is
antichrist;" and whosoever does not confess
the testimony of the cross, is of the devil;

and whosoever perverts the oracles of the
Lord to his own lusts, and says that there is
neither a resurrection nor a judgment, he is
the first-born of Satan.[45]

Again, all that Polycarp says here is based on
Scripture and the understanding of the apostles.
These are the Christian beliefs, upheld against
Gnosticism, which claimed that the flesh was bad, so
Jesus could not have been fully human. By saying
that, the Gnostics destroyed the effectiveness of Jesus'
sacrifice, for if He had not been human, His sacrifice
would not have applied to humanity.

In one way, those who did not hold to Christian
doctrine did the church a favor. The early church
had to hammer out what it believed as it defended
the faith handed down by the apostles. As long as
the early church leaders held to the teachings of
Scripture, they made good decisions. Those who
wanted to add to the faith or water it down did
Christianity no favors—and before long they wan-
dered off into ideas that could not be found in
Scripture and became no longer Christian.

The church vigorously defended itself against such error. It examined the teachings of the apostles and the teachings of those whose beliefs differed. In doing so, the very early church created an orthodoxy that held tight to the Scriptures. For the first few centuries, Christian doctrine stuck to the critical elements of the faith. And as long as Christianity focused on that, it was strong. Only later, as the church grew in political importance, did other elements begin to creep in. The basic truths were still there, but they sometimes became obliterated by other ideas or focuses.

In Christianity, . . .the answer to bad theology can never be no theology. It must be good theology.[46]

Even today, real Christianity holds to the ideas in the Apostles' Creed. The theology that developed around the creed was strong and defensible. It tells us just who Jesus is.

It's up to you whether you decide to make this creed your own. If you decide to accept what the creed says—if you decide to believe the evidence that supports Jesus' case—what will that mean for you personally? In the next half of the book, I'll try to answer that question.

Part II

WHAT DOES IT MEAN TO BELIEVE IN JESUS?

6

MEETING JESUS

Why does it matter if I meet Jesus?
What does it take to meet Him?

Fine, you may be saying to yourself. *You have a good argument for Jesus. But what does that mean to me? After all, isn't any other religious figure just as good as Jesus? Don't they all believe in the same things?*

No.

You've seen the testimony Jesus gave of Himself. No other religious leader has claimed what He claimed. No person on earth has done what He has done. No other religion has been so reviled, stood on its head intellectually, and still remained strong.

Have you ever said to yourself, "I am impressed with the wonderful truths of God's Word, but He can't really expect me to live up to that and work all those details into my life!"... We think His ideals are lofty and they impress us, but we believe He is not in touch with reality—that what He says cannot actually be done.... My misgivings arise from the fact that I search within to find how He will do what He says. My doubts spring from the depths of my own inferiority.[47]

Today more Christians are being persecuted for their faith than ever before in history, yet they still hold onto their faith. Why would anyone do that?

Persecuted Christians don't hold fast because their faith has a good argument—though it does. They don't lose all they own because it makes sense that Jesus is God. They do it because Jesus has had an impact on their lives that no other idea or leader has had. They do it for love.

A Hole in the Heart

St. Augustine commented that humans have a hole

in the heart that only God can fill. Without God, most people reach a point where they feel empty and useless. They wonder what life is about, and their existence may seem purposeless. They find things to fill the emptiness, from jobs that take most of their lives to a string of relationships that never quite seem to work. But the emptiness remains.

The Bible tells us why we feel this hollowness. "For by him all things were created: things in heaven and on earth, visible and invisible. . .all things were created by him and for him" (Colossians 1:16). We were created for God, and only He can fill that empty spot inside our hearts. Our lives feel purposeless until we have connected with the Creator. We desperately need His love, but like lost children, we wander far from it.

Have you ever heard someone complain that she had too much love? Probably not. Man, woman, and child, we tend to search for more love in our lives— and often we do not find it. Even our pets have a never-ending need for affection.

So often we look for love in the wrong places— in faulty relationships or drugs and drink or by expecting too much of the wrong people. We end up disappointed, wishing there were a relationship that did not fail us.

There *is* a relationship that will not fail—one with God. Relating to such a Being may have its challenges. It may require much from us, but it returns more than we could expect—more than any human relationship could provide.

The last chapter mentioned reconciliation with God. You may become reconciled *to* an idea, accepting something you're not really keen on, but you can only be reconciled *with* another person. God is not just an idea or theory, floating out in space; in Jesus, it becomes abundantly clear that God has a personality too. He has the ability to relate to people. He created Adam and Eve to be close to Him, then He made covenants with succeeding generations. From the beginning of creation, He led people into deeper relationships with Himself. With Jesus, God gave a concrete view of Himself that we could relate to in a way we'd never done before.

As a child, I went to Sunday school often, but I never received this message. God was a distant being. I had no intimate relationship with Him, and it never crossed my mind that one was even available. God was "way up there," and I was "down here." Our paths hardly seemed to cross. That's the way many people feel—distant and uninterested in God, except as a vague idea or a philosophy. Or they may see Him as a judge, ready to pounce on any error of thought or conduct.

People feel that way until they meet Jesus and understand that He wants us to have a real relationship with Him—one where we can share both our hurts and joys. It's a relationship that offers strength and comfort, not just divine judgment.

Perhaps this is a new idea to you. You've seen God as distant and uncaring or ready to expose all your mistakes. That's not the message Jesus came to tell you. It's not the message of the Bible.

Filling the Hole

God doesn't want us to feel empty inside. Our emptiness is simply the natural result of leaving God out of our lives. He created us to relate to Him, but we have gone our own way instead.

Though God desperately wants a relationship

with people, He does not force it on us. He holds out His arms and draws us to Himself, but we have a part to play too. We have to accept all that God has done for us through Jesus. Faith in Jesus is a gift, though, not God's great demand of humanity.

Jesus' death on the cross was designed to do for us the thing we could never do for ourselves: eradicate wrongdoing—or sin—from our lives. That includes all our wrong thoughts and actions, the unintentional mistakes we made—anything that is not right, pure, and good. We've known that we haven't always done right, whether we've gotten involved in "serious" sins or led a fairly upright life. If we're honest with ourselves, we know we've fallen short.

If you have wronged a friend or family member, it's hard to feel close. You don't feel as if you want to be in that person's company until things are made right. It's the same with God. We keep waiting for the other shoe to fall—we feel uncomfortable and distant, waiting for retribution—until we know things are made right.

Jesus, Thy blood and righteousness
My beauty are, my glorious dress;

'Midst flaming worlds, in these arrayed,
With joy shall I lift up my head.

Nicolaus L. von Zinzendorf

Jesus makes things right. He stepped in and paid the price for our sin when He died on the cross. So in an amazing way, when we recognize that He died for our wrongdoing and ask Him to take over our lives and help us to live rightly, He will. He reconciles us with God the Father by taking all of our sins on Himself.

The conversion experience is different for each person. Some people slowly come to the realization that they need God's forgiveness. Over time, they simply know that they believe that Jesus' sacrifice was for them. We're not talking a general assent here, an "I'm okay, Jesus is okay" kind of idea, but a whole-hearted, heartfelt belief. For others of us, this trans-action takes place at a certain place, at a specific time. Suddenly we're confronted by the facts of our sin and the price Jesus paid for it. We want freedom from our messed-up lives so badly that we can almost taste it.

Long my imprisoned spirit lay,
Fast bound in sin and nature's night.

Thine eye diffused a quickening ray:
I woke—the dungeon flamed with light!
My chains fell off, my heart was free,
I rose, went forth, and followed thee.

Charles Wesley

How faith comes to our hearts does not matter. What matters is only that it *does* come. Those who accept Jesus' sacrifice change their eternal destiny (Matthew 19:29; John 14:1–4). Suddenly, they are heaven bound.

When we stand before God, in judgment, Jesus can either claim us as His followers or deny any relationship at all. If we acknowledge Him on earth, He will acknowledge us—if we deny Him, we will be denied, and hell will be our eternal home.

God didn't send Jesus into this world to condemn you, but to save you.

> For God did not send his Son into the world to condemn the world, but to save the world through him. Whoever believes in him is not condemned, but whoever does not believe stands condemned already

because he has not believed in the name of
God's one and only Son (John 3:17–18).

Before You Say No

God won't drag you into heaven, kicking and scream-
ing. You don't have to go. People through the centuries have turned Jesus' offer down. So what if you
do say no?

As clear as Jesus was about heaven, He was
equally clear about hell. The hell He described was
not a party place, but one of torment and darkness (Revelation 20:10; Matthew 8:12). Unlike the
nice, comfortable view of an afterlife without God
that many people have, Jesus did not describe it as a
place for only "really bad" people, like Hitler. He
never said that anyone who did her best or made
every effort he could to follow all the rules would get
an entrance pass into heaven. Instead, He warned
His disciples that unless they could do better than
the Pharisees, Israel's best rule keepers, they would
not enter the kingdom of heaven (Matthew 5:20).
Then He asked the Pharisees how they could escape

being condemned to hell (Matthew 23:33).

Trying hard isn't good enough. Even the strenuous rules the Pharisees added to the biblical ones were not enough to strain every sin from their lives.

Jesus taught:

> "You have heard that it was said to the people long ago, 'Do not murder, and anyone who murders will be subject to judgment.' But I tell you that anyone who is angry with his brother will be subject to judgment. Again, anyone who says to his brother, 'Raca,' is answerable to the Sanhedrin. But anyone who says, 'You fool!' will be in danger of the fire of hell (Matthew 5:21–22).

Here Jesus expanded on the Old Testament commandment against murder, to get to the heart of what God meant. The Pharisees thought that because they'd never stabbed or poisoned their neighbors, they were in the clear of sin. But Jesus told them that a person didn't have to commit murder to be worthy of God's judgment. Behind any murder is the anger that led to the violence—sin in the heart led to the physical act. Someone who called another "Empty Head" (the probable meaning for "Raca"), wishing another ill with what we could consider a mild rebuke, is not worthy of living in heaven beside a perfect God who cannot tolerate sin. And who among us has never called another something that meant "fool"? According to this standard, we all deserve to go to hell.

But it doesn't have to be that way. That's not the way God wanted it. According to Jesus' claims about Himself, God sent Him to die for an impossibly confused and tainted humanity. The only way God could cover over humanity's sin was with the perfect sacrifice of a man who had no sin—and that meant He had to be God, because all humans err. The solution was Jesus.

You can spend eternity in misery or a blissful relationship with Jesus. It's your choice. If you know you have not come to God and recognized the need for his forgiveness, now is as good a time as any. Don't delay if you feel God tugging at your heart. Why put off the start of the most wonderful relationship possible?

As I did, you may simply pour out your need and contrition in your own words. Or, if you want to, use the following words to express yourself to God:

> Lord God, I know I haven't lived the way
> You want me to. I've sinned against You.
> Thank You for sending Jesus to die on the cross
> so that my sins could be forgiven. Please forgive
> me now and help me live for You.

When I prayed a prayer much like that, I felt as if I had opened a door and saw the heavenly sunlight pouring through. I felt all clean and new. There was no doubt in my mind or heart that God had done as He promises in Romans 6:4: He had given me new life. I was a new creation (2 Corinthians 5:17). Not everyone feels that way immediately. Some new Christians don't feel much of a change. But as they trust God and begin to follow Him, new life springs up in them.

Some people make that decision in church, when they walk down an aisle to publicly claim Jesus as their Savior. Some do it in a private place. The where or how doesn't make a difference; what does make a difference is the open heart that accepts God. That's the door to reconciliation with Him. We've been converted to a new life, and it starts a new relationship with Him.

> **Conversion is not repairing of the old building; but it takes down and erects a new structure. The sincere Christian is quite a new fabric, from the foundation to the topstone all new.**
> **Joseph Alleine**

This new life is what the martyrs died for, what persecuted believers today stand firm for. Polycarp, bishop of Smyrna, faced death for his faith, because he would not worship Caesar. Though the governor pled with him to give in, Polycarp stood firm and answered, "For the eighty-six years I have served Him, He has never done me any ill; how can I blaspheme my Saviour and my King?"[48] The gift of new life and a relationship with Jesus, the Son of God, was worth dying for.

Starting a New Life

If you've asked God for forgiveness because of what Jesus has done for you, He has given you a wonderful new gift. But what if you just put it on a shelf and ignore it? It won't be long before that gift seems tarnished and useless. To keep the freshness in your new life, you have to live for God, not for yourself. This means facing challenges and doubts squarely, trusting that God will keep your new life growing. Being a Christian is often described as a "Christian walk." You are in this for the long haul, but you can make it if you take every step with God.

Whatever the challenge, God can keep you faithful. But you have a part in this too. We'll look at that in the next chapter.

7

WHAT DO I DO NOW THAT I'M A CHRISTIAN?

What does it mean to live the Christian life?

If you've made the decision to accept all that Christ has done for you, what now? Will life be different— or will you just go along in the same path? What can you expect?

When Scripture promises new life, it means it! From his own experience, the apostle Paul could say, "If anyone is in Christ, he is a new creation; the old has gone, the new has come!" (2 Corinthians 5:17). The change, as Paul goes on to tell us, is not in our imaginations. We have not dreamed something or had a wild imaginary journey. Though we may wake up the next day and ask ourselves, *Was it real?* we will soon have no doubts. The change is permanent, if we've meant what we told God. He has done it all—reconciling us to Himself through Jesus.

If that change were just up to us, it might last a short time, but it wouldn't make long-term alterations in our lives. Before long, we'd slip back into our old ruts. But just as a child can hold tenaciously onto life, grow, and become stronger, the new Christian, motivated by love for God, can reach out into new things, change, and develop into the person God designed him or her to become.

We believe that the first time we're born, as children, it's human life given to us; and when we accept Jesus as our Savior, it's a new life. That's what "born again" means.

Jimmy Carter

Starting the New Life

But just as a baby needs care and attention, our new Christian lives cannot be ignored. To some degree, what we put into them, from the moment of our first decision, will dictate what we experience spiritually.

Stefan walked down the aisle and made a commitment to Jesus—but from that day on you never would have known it. He continued to be a "party" guy and never went to church or even talked about Christ with his Christian friends. Unless things change at some point, Stefan will probably get what he gave to the Christian life. Since he has never stood up for Jesus, he probably didn't make a real commitment, and in heaven, Jesus may not stand up for him (Luke 12:8–9; John 3:18; Matthew 25:41).

Ruth had a slow start in her new faith. She came to Christ through a tract she found in a hospital. For a long time she floundered, but finally she found a church and began attending as often as possible. Slowly, as she began to read her Bible and learn about her faith, Ruth began to see changes in her life. Today she is a strong Christian, but if she had it to do over again, she would have connected with a church sooner.

Chuck came to Christ and immediately started to grow. He attended a strong youth group and a Bible-believing church. Quickly, his life began to change, and within a short time he was sure that God had called him to the ministry. You might call him a fast-track Christian.

God works differently in individual Christians' lives. We don't all grow at the same rate or have the same experiences, but God expects us to mature in faith. Different growth schedules are no excuse for laziness! To make the most of your new life, jump right in with both feet.

As a new Christian, realize that what happened was not a one-time event that requires nothing more of you. Jesus warned that in the end some people who thought they had claimed faith in Him will be disappointed:

"Not everyone who says to me, 'Lord, Lord,' will enter the kingdom of heaven, but only he who does the will of my Father who is in heaven. Many will say to me on that day,

'Lord, Lord, did we not prophesy in your name, and in your name drive out demons and perform many miracles?' Then I will tell them plainly, 'I never knew you. Away from me, you evildoers!' " (Matthew 7:21–23).

Being a Christian means doing God's will, not ignoring it and then, like Stefan, expecting all the benefits Jesus offers those who tenaciously follow Him. That's what Christians sometimes refer to as "fire insurance" Christianity—some people accept Christ because they are afraid of hell even though they don't really want to step foot in heaven. It doesn't work.

What is man's primary purpose?
Man's primary purpose is to glorify God and to enjoy him forever.[49]

Doing God's will may sound simple in theory, but living as a Christian has its challenges. Not everyone will like the fact that you now belong to Christ. You can expect some people to challenge your new faith. And making changes in your life isn't always easy. The good news is that you can go beyond these challenges, if you trust God and continue to follow Him. He will give you the strength, through His Spirit:

> Those who live in accordance with the Spirit have their minds set on what the Spirit desires. The mind of sinful man is death, but the mind controlled by the Spirit is life and peace. . . . You, however, are controlled not by the sinful nature but by the Spirit, if the Spirit of God lives in you. And if anyone does not have the Spirit of Christ, he does not belong to Christ (Romans 8:5–6, 9).

Let God's Spirit control you, and you will have a happy and successful Christian life.

> **Many of us have a picture of what a Christian should be, and looking at this image in other Christians' lives becomes a hindrance to our focusing on God. This is not salvation—it is not simple enough. He says, in effect, "Look to Me and you are saved," not "You will be saved someday." We will find what we are looking for if we will concentrate on Him.**[50]

If you accepted Jesus, He has given you His Spirit. But you can choose to ignore the Spirit's gentle whisper (1 Kings 19:12). You have invited Him to the door of your life, but Jesus will not barge in. He waits to be invited to change your life. All you have to do is ask, in prayer, and be willing to obey His commands.

Making the Most of Your New Life

Paul spoke of the believer's new life when he told the Ephesian church: "You were taught, with regard to your former way of life, to put off your old self, which is being corrupted by its deceitful desires; to be made new in the attitude of your minds; and to put on the new self, created to be like God in true righteousness and holiness" (Ephesians 4:22–24). The new life is not something that develops without effort. Believers can decide not to do much of anything, like Stefan, to grow slowly, like Ruth, or jump into the faith with both feet, like Chuck. But God designed us for change, when we accept Him. He wants us to become like Him, and we won't do that if we remain stuck in our old attitudes and actions.

Paul admonished the believers in the Colossian church: "Do not lie to each other, since you have taken off your old self with its practices and have put on the new self, which is being renewed in knowledge in the image of its Creator" (Colossians 3:9–10). So what practices do you have to take off, and what will you replace them with?

Reading the Guidebook

If you were expecting a quick list of rules and regulations that will help you be a good Christian, I'm afraid I can't offer you that. It didn't work for the Pharisees, and it won't work today. But God does offer you a Guidebook—His Word, the Bible. In it you will find a lifetime's worth of help and direction. God gave it to you to help you know what will please Him, so you can put off the wrong things and replace them with right actions, thoughts, and words.

What authority from God directs us how to glorify and enjoy Him?
The only authority for glorifying and enjoying

Him is the Bible, which is the word of God and is made up of the Old and New Testaments.[51]

Choosing a Bible

If you have come to Christ through a friend, your friend may give you a Bible. But if you have not been given one, buy one for yourself, at a bookstore. A Christian bookstore will provide you with the widest choice, and there you can ask for help, from a person who knows something about the different translations. But if you feel more confident, any chain bookstore and many independent bookstores will offer at least a few Bibles.

Do not try to order on-line, unless you have the help of an experienced Christian. I went on-line with one large distributor, entered *Bible,* and got a list of over 173,000 books, very few of which were really Bibles. *Holy Bible* was better, but the list was still fairly endless. If you order on-line, you also will not get to take a look at what you are getting beforehand. (Besides, you will have to wait for your order instead of immediately beginning to read.)

Sin will keep you from this Book. This Book will keep you from sin.

Dwight L. Moody

There are many Bible translations available. For new Christians, one that is easy to read is important. Take a few minutes to glance through and see if you are comfortable with the language of the translation. Is it too hard or too easy for your usual reading level? You want something that feels comfortable.

The King James Bible is a favorite of many people, but unless you are already connected with a church that uses that version exclusively, you will probably want something more modern. The King James Version, translated in the early seventeenth century, is a verbal challenge for most Christians today. It was translated around the era in which William Shakespeare was writing, so unless you comprehend his plays easily, you will probably not find this the simplest translation to understand. If you look at a copy of the King James Version and have trouble with the vocabulary, but you are connected with a church that uses only this version of the Bible, you may wish to purchase a second, easier-to-read version for your personal reading time. In time you will become familiar with the King James Version as well.

There are many Bibles out there. The New King James Bible is based on the King James Version, but with much more modern language. It is easier to read, and many people enjoy it. You might also like the New International Version, which is often used in churches, or the New American Standard Version, which is a highly accurate translation, but one that occasionally sacrifices readability for translation accuracy. The New Living Translation offers the Bible in the fresh, informal language we speak today. The differences between these versions relate to theological interpretations and ease of use, but generally all these translations will give you a basic understanding of Jesus. Later, if you join a church that uses another version, you can always purchase that one as well.

Starting to Read

Most new Christians find the Bible daunting. Someone places a huge book in their hands, and they don't know where to start. Many open to the beginning, the Book of Genesis. If they manage to wade through that, and perhaps Exodus, they bog down in Numbers, with its lists of unfamiliar names. The Old Testament is wonderful, but much of it is strange to us. Read all of it, but don't begin with it.

A better place to start is in the New Testament. Most people who are unfamiliar with Scripture relate better to this part of the Bible. The Gospels, the first four books of the New Testament, tell the life story of Jesus. Reading one of them is a good place to begin. If you have another Christian guiding your Bible study, follow his or her advice on which Gospel to choose. Otherwise, begin with either Mark or John. Mark, the first Gospel to be written, gives you a brief, intense view of Jesus' ministry. John's Gospel provides an almost heavenly vision of Jesus, one that includes stories that are not in the other Gospels. If you are Jewish, you may wish to begin with the Book of Matthew, which was written to the Jews. But whichever you read, once you are done, go on to read the other Gospels. Remember that Matthew, Mark, and Luke follow Jesus' ministry more or less chronologically. They are very similar in the stories they tell, but they will give slightly different perspectives and information. To get a fuller picture, you may want to compare similar passages, as you get deeper into Bible study.

The first time you read the Bible, accept that you will not understand everything. It is a large book, with much information in it. Your first read-through will be merely to let you know what is there and give you some basic understanding. You're simply getting familiar with Scripture. Don't demand of yourself that you understand every word. This is a book you will be studying for a lifetime, and no book that valuable can be understood without years of study. Even lifelong Bible scholars find new truth in it every time they read it again.

When you have finished the Gospels, I'd suggest that you read the Book of Acts, which is Luke's history of the early church. Then read the letters—Romans through Jude. Finally, read Revelation, the last Book of the New Testament. When you are done with that, begin the Old Testament.

If you prefer to study sections of the Old and New Testament together, there are many reading programs for going through the Scriptures in a year—or more, if you want to move more slowly. You may prefer to use one of these, if someone in your church points you to a good one.

> **The Bible touches on a variety of controversial top-**
> **ics. . . . In spite of its diversity there is one story, one**
> **theme, one solution, and one plan of redemption for**
> **mankind.**[52]

I vividly remember my first reading of the Bible. I began because a friend commented that I could hardly know what I believed in, if I had not read the Bible. So I began to read, feeling rather confused but determined to get all the way through. Though I didn't break any speed records, eventually I completed the whole thing. Sometimes I plodded through the Old Testament passages, barely knowing what they were talking about. But by the time I reached the prophet Isaiah, something funny started to happen. I began to understand passages that I'd read in other places. All of a sudden, I was connecting other Old and New Testament texts with what I was reading. The Bible had begun to make sense to me.

At some point, if you keep reading, the Bible will "click" for you, too. You will not fully understand the entire book—no one does—but you'll begin to have a feel for it. Your biblical understanding will grow from there.

As you read, apply what you are reading to your

own walk with Jesus. When Paul admonishes a church to avoid a sin, is it something that's in your life? Take his words to heart and pray, asking God to help you overcome that sin. Then make efforts to avoid it in your life.

That brings us to another way your spiritual life can grow—prayer.

Talking with God

Just as you can't have a close relationship with someone you never talk to, you won't draw very close to God if you never say a word to Him or listen to His response. Prayer is your way of communicating with God.

Remember, God wants a relationship with you. When the relationship does not seem smooth, you may not feel like talking. But God always wants to know what is going on in your heart and mind. "Cast all your anxiety on him because he cares for you," Peter tells us (1 Peter 5:7). When you are worried or bothered by something, God cares about it and wants to hear about it from you—even if you're struggling with something about Him or His Word. And when you are happy, that's a great time to share your joy with God.

There are many guides for prayer out there. Make use of them, if you wish. Anything that helps you draw close to God is fine. But don't get so bogged down in a method of praying that you lose sight of the One to whom you are praying. Sometimes methods make us think there is only one "right" way to pray, and we focus on the *how,* not the *who*—Jesus.

Though it's simple, the best advice on prayer that I've ever received is to speak to God as a friend. Develop your relationship with Him. Tell Him all your troubles—let Him know when you are mad at Him, instead of acting as if He was "way up there" and would not understand. He does understand, even if He doesn't do things your way. One important thing to remember about God is that He cannot be manipulated. You will not be able to bend Him to your will, but He will always do what is best for you.

For the first part of my Christian life, when I did not understand whatever was going on in my life, I'd approach God with the words, "But, Lord!" To some this might seem irreverent, but I was trying, as a young Christian, to understand the Christian life. God didn't always explain the whys, and I didn't stop at the "but" and forget that He was Lord—I followed

His way even when it seemed confusing. We were in this relationship together.

At the time, I wondered if my questioning *was* irreverent. But I knew I was being honest with God. Not until later in my walk did I realize how important that honesty had been. Through it, I began to see I could trust God with my questions and negative feelings. So don't be afraid to tell God just how you feel!

Approach God as one who cares and helps, not as one who hurts you. Hurts will come in life; we all suffer them, but God can turn even the worst event into a plan for good. " 'For I know the plans I have for you,' declares the LORD, 'plans to prosper you and not to harm you, plans to give you hope and a future' " (Jeremiah 29:11).

After you've prayed, take time to listen to God's response. Perhaps you will immediately see a solution to a question you've been pondering, but it doesn't always happen so quickly. God may take time to answer; still, if you listen and seek, your answer will come. "Ask and it will be given to you; seek and you will find; knock and the door will be opened to you," said Jesus. "For everyone who asks receives; he who seeks finds; and to him who knocks, the door will be opened" (Matthew 7:7–8).

Sometimes you will ask more than once. This passage seems to show a growing intensity—first asking, then seeking, then knocking at heaven's door to find the answer. God does not always give the response you'd like to hear. He may not hand you all you want, at this moment, but He will answer. Sometimes the answer is "No" or "Wait," but God will always be there for you, with the best solution to any problem.

Communing with the Faithful

Reading the Bible and praying are large parts of the personal side of faith. I've begun with them because, even if you don't have a Christian friend to help you or a church that teaches the Bible, you can get started in the faith on your own. But don't settle for "lone ranger" Christianity. It's a very unsatisfying way to relate to God. God made you to connect with other Christians—it's the only way you can accomplish all He's intended for you to do. So get together with people you know are Christians. Start looking for a good church, if you don't have one. You can read more about how to do that in chapter 9.

8

WHAT HAPPENS IF
I FAIL JESUS?

**Sooner or later, human beings always fail.
How does human failure affect
our relationship with Jesus?**

Jose met Jesus, and everything in the world seemed
fine. *Could life be any better?* he asked himself. He was
thrilled that he'd become a Christian.

For about a month everything seemed perfect—
until the night he got into a fight with one of the
guys at his Bible study. The next day Jose felt embarrassed—he didn't even want to talk to God about it,

and how could he face his friends at Bible study again? Had he completely forgotten what Jesus had done for him? Had he lost his salvation? He'd failed God so miserably.

Many new Christians have a honeymoon period when they feel so close to God that they doubt it will ever change. Their spiritual lives go unusually well. Even the "secular" parts of their lives may seem to thrive. But before long the honeymoon ends, and they discover what it takes to truly follow Christ.

That's what happened to Jose. God had shown him what it was like to have a successful Christian walk, but many things could keep Jose from living like that permanently. The wrong attitudes he'd held before he became a Christian were forgiven but not magically eradicated. Jose would have to learn how, with God's help, to make enduring changes in his life.

The Sin That So Entangles

Becoming a Christian is a supernatural event, but it is not "magic." God doesn't immediately wipe away everything we've done wrong and release us from responsibility for our pre-Christian thoughts and actions. He doesn't make our lives perfect in one swift swoop.

> **The origin of sin is a mystery and must for ever remain such to us. . . . For some reason God has permitted sin to enter this world, and that is all we know. His permitting it, however, in no way makes God the author of sin.**[53]

Why doesn't God "zap" us into perfection? Because He loves us. If God magically cleaned up our lives, perhaps it would seem so easy that we'd never appreciate it, or maybe the change would be so great that we'd never be able to handle it. The impact of that sudden change on our lives might be superficial, and if there's one thing you can say about God, it's that He's not superficial.

So then, you may be wondering, *has God really forgiven my sin? Is it really, as Psalm 103:12 says, as far as the east is from the west?*

Christians Still Sin

God has kept His promises—our sin *is* forgiven when we believe in Jesus. But all of us still live on earth and still struggle with things such as error, wrongdoing, and bad attitudes. We hold onto the promise of sinlessness in heaven, even as we fight the remnants of sin that remain active in our lives.

The spiritually great Paul, who brought the good news of Jesus' salvation to people of many nations, described his personal struggle with sin:

> I am unspiritual, sold as a slave to sin.
> I do not understand what I do. For what
> I want to do I do not do, but what I hate I
> do. . . . It is no longer I myself who do it, but
> it is sin living in me. I know that nothing
> good lives in me, that is, in my sinful nature.
> For I have the desire to do what is good, but
> I cannot carry it out. For what I do is not
> the good I want to do; no, the evil I do not
> want to do—this I keep on doing. Now if I
> do what I do not want to do, it is no longer
> I who do it, but it is sin living in me that

does it (Romans 7:14–15, 17–20).

Paul had a keen awareness of the damage sin did to the spirit, and he knew his need to avoid it. All the while he struggled with sin, Paul knew deep inside that he wanted to obey God. But even for this spiritual giant this was hard work. Even he could not seem to do it perfectly.

Some Christians explain this dichotomy by saying that "positionally" you are saved and perfect. That means that in heaven, God has completed the transaction. He has brought you into His kingdom and enabled you to do good. You are in position in heaven, even when you still struggle with sin on earth.

Paul explained this part of God's role in forgiveness when he told the Romans:

> Therefore, there is now no condemnation for those who are in Christ Jesus, because through Christ Jesus the law of the Spirit of life set me free from the law of sin and death. For what the law was powerless to do in that it was weakened by the sinful nature, God did by sending his own Son in

the likeness of sinful man to be a sin offering (Romans 8:1–3).

If God no longer condemns us, why do we still have a problem? Have we really changed at all?

> My sin—O, the bliss of the glorious thought,
> My sin—not in part but the whole,
> Is nailed to the cross and I bear it no more,
> Praise the Lord, praise the Lord, O my soul!
>
> Horatio G. Spafford

Do You Care About Sin?

Before you became a Christian, sin probably wasn't a big issue. Occasionally you might feel sorry if you wronged someone, but you didn't feel deep sorrow that often or long. You weren't fully aware of your sin or its consequences. Now you may feel as if you are supersensitive to many things you do wrong.

The apostle John described the difference between the non-Christian and the Christian when he said, "If we claim to be without sin [that's the non-Christian], we deceive ourselves and the truth is not in us. If we confess our sins [that's the Christian], he is faithful and just and will forgive us our sins and purify us from all unrighteousness" (1 John 1:8–9). Before we knew Christ, we didn't care that we sinned, but now, alert to sin's consequences, we turn to God and ask His forgiveness. As we do that, He begins to purify us from sin—but it's a process, not a bit of magic. We take part in daily purification by obeying God with our thoughts, words, and deeds. Though, like Paul, we may always feel the temptation to sin, we begin to overcome it, as God continues to make us more like Jesus.

Overcoming Sin

Perhaps you've heard non-Christians complain that Christians are such hypocrites—they say all these high-minded things, then never live up to them. If the complainers are looking for perfection, that may be true—no Christian has lived perfectly, because sin still exists here on earth. But committed Christians no longer feel satisfied with sin. They seek to become more like Christ and tolerate less and less sin in their lives. They may not be perfect, but they are works in progress that are improving day by day.

Paul told the Romans how to make this improvement happen, "Count yourselves dead to sin but alive to God in Christ Jesus. Therefore do not let sin reign in your mortal body so that you obey its evil desires" (Romans 6:11–12). The same apostle whom we saw lamenting his own sin knew that the solution was to fight back against it. He gave the Romans hope by telling them they could offer their bodies to God instead of the devil, and because they were under God's grace, sin would no longer master them (Romans 6:11–14).

If we just sit back in our Christian lives and wait for God to make us perfect, we'll be disappointed. God expects us to take part in the change. But we can't do it in our own power, either. God's Spirit makes the change in us, not our own efforts. Before we were Christians, no matter how hard we tried, we could never get it right, and we still can't unless we rely on God and let Him empower us to change. As we confess sin to Him and seek His help in putting it out of our lives, He will give us victory over it, little by little.

Those Who Give Up the Fight

We can choose to ignore sin or we can vigorously attack it. By ignoring it, we will almost assure our own frustration with Jesus. Christians were meant to grow, and when they don't, they may begin to feel that Christianity "doesn't work."

Of course Christianity won't work if you don't join in the fight. That's what faith is—a battle against sin (1 Timothy 1:18). Those who stay on the sidelines will never have successful spiritual lives—they will shipwreck their faith (1 Timothy 1:19).

Fighting the Good Fight

"Love the Lord your God with all your heart and with all your soul and with all your mind and with all your strength," Jesus told the teachers of the law (Mark 12:30). That's a huge demand! But that's what overcoming sin takes. We can't just pussyfoot with sin, avoiding it one day and succumbing to its temptations the next. Such an attitude gets us nowhere.

With All Your Heart

Jeremiah warns, "Judah's sin is engraved with an iron tool. . .on the tablets of their hearts. . . . The heart is deceitful above all things and beyond cure" (Jeremiah 17:1, 9). On our own, we cannot change our hearts and make them good, anymore than the prophet Jeremiah could change the hearts of the people of his nation.

Out of the overflow of the heart the mouth speaks.
Matthew 12:34

What is the solution? How can our hearts change? If we too pray Jeremiah's prayer, "Heal me, O LORD, and I will be healed; save me and I will be saved, for you are the one I praise" (Jeremiah 17:14), God can help us understand our deceitful hearts. People may help us in our Christian walks, but God is the only one who knows every cranny of our hearts. And He creates new hearts. The psalmist asked, "Create in me a pure heart, O God, and renew a steadfast spirit within me" (Psalm 51:10).

Be Thou my Vision, O Lord of my heart;
Naught be all else to me, save that Thou art —
Thou my best thought, by day or by night,
Waking or sleeping, Thy presence my light.

Ancient Irish hymn

That's why many Christians can testify to real life-style changes after their conversions. I saw an example of this when I met Art. Before becoming a Christian, he had been very deeply and ritually involved in the occult. But one day someone witnessed to him, God tugged at his heart, and he knew he had to accept Christ—immediately. When I met Art a few years later, his life no longer focused on evil; I have never seen anyone so totally sold out to God. He knew the price of turning to Satan, and his commitment was thorough. Someone who had known Art before his conversion could hardly believe such a change had occurred in this tough guy. But for the years I had contact with Art, he consistently lived out his Christian walk. We only lost touch when he moved away to become involved in a Christian ministry.

With All Your Soul

God has made a soul change in us. Though we can feel the desires of our hearts alter, that old sin nature keeps nipping at us. Like Paul, while we'd like to give up sin, it still permeates our beings.

John Newton, author of the favorite hymn "Amazing Grace," understood what it meant to have sin delay his spiritual life. Before he knew Christ, John was involved in sailing ships that carried African slaves to the Americas. It was a degrading thing both for the slaves and Newton, who became known for his blasphemy, which included ridiculing the gospel.

In March, 1748, while sailing in a very heavy storm, Newton so feared for his life that he became aware of his own deep sinfulness. Doubtful of his own ability to be saved, he barely managed to call on God—but God answered. Newton had yet to fully believe, however, because: "The comfortless principles of infidelity were deeply riveted, and I rather wished than believe [sic] these things [the scriptural truths] were real facts."[54]

I can see no reason why the Lord singled me out for mercy, but this, "that it seemed good to him;" unless it was to shew, by one astonishing instance that with him "nothing is impossible."[55]

For a considerable time, Newton was not fully committed to God, but at last he wrote that "with the greatest solemnity [I] engaged myself to be the Lord's for ever, and only his. This was not a formal but a sincere surrender, under a warm sense of mercies recently received."[56]

Newton continued to captain slave ships until 1754. Though he treated slaves in his vessel with more kindness than most, he did not change his career. During this time his spiritual walk seems to have been fairly barren. But in 1755 ill health forced him to cease sailing, and he became a tide surveyor. For the next five years evangelical preachers George Whitefield and John Wesley influenced the ex-captain, and his serious growth as a Christian began. While he worked as a surveyor Newton began studying Latin, and in 1764 he became a priest in the Church of England. He also became involved in the British antislavery movement.

Poet William Cowper came to hear Newton

preach, and a friendship grew between them. The new priest and his nearby neighbor began a collection called *Olney Hymns*. Newton wrote 280 of the 348 hymns, which include "Amazing Grace" and "Glorious Things of Thee Are Spoken."

> Amazing grace! How sweet the sound—
> That saved a wretch like me!
> I once was lost but now am found,
> Was blind but now I see.
>
> John Newton

Newton's slow start and long period of doubts slowed down his spiritual life—but he nevertheless went on to become a strong Christian whose words have influenced countless people.

As a new Christian, you know that God has only just started with you. Don't let sin turn you from Him! God is even now working to claim every scrap of your soul for Himself.

Don't separate yourself from the things that will help you grow in your faith, as Newton did. Become involved with a good church, read the Scriptures, pray often, and seek God's will in your life. God wants to change your life, but He will not force Himself on you. You have to willingly give yourself over to Him. Whether you stay in the slave ship or start on a new career with Him is your option.

The psalmist testified: "The Lord. . .restores my soul. He guides me in paths of righteousness for his name's sake" (Psalm 23:1, 3). When we trust in God, He begins to conform us to the likeness of His Son (Romans 8:29). God has begun to rework your life. Although you will not instantaneously reach perfection, enjoy the lifelong walk with Him that will change your soul.

With All Your Mind

Can you claim never to have thought something wrong about a friend, family member, or acquaintance? Letting God take full control of your thoughts, so that you can act according to His will, can be a great challenge. After all, each of us acts on the things we think. Ideas, good or evil, have to pass through our brains before we can do anything about them.

With God in control of our minds, these dark

thoughts may still flash into our heads, but they do not have to take up residence there. Through His Spirit, which brings forgiveness to our hearts, we can allow God control.

Corrie ten Boom had experienced actions that came from the worst thinking of the twentieth century. During World War II she spent months in concentration camps, because she and her family had hidden Jews from the Nazi invaders of her homeland, Holland. Her elderly father died in German custody, ten days after his arrest. Her sister Betsie died later in a camp. The horrors the sisters experienced at the hands of the Germans make a harrowing tale. But from her experiences, Corrie learned that Jesus is Victor. That truth became a theme in her speaking and writing after the war.

Ten years after Betsie's death, Corrie met a nurse who had been cruel to her sister as she was dying in the concentration camp. As soon as Corrie recognized the woman, hatred swept into her heart. Following the war, Corrie had begun speaking to many Germans of God's love and forgiveness, and here she was harboring such hatred. Swiftly, she asked God's forgiveness and help to love her enemies.

Because she believed that even in this Jesus could be Victor, instead of harboring hatred in her mind, Corrie led that nurse to Jesus.[62]

The quiet mind is richer than a crown.

Robert Greene

This was not the first person who had harmed her and her family whom Corrie met after the war—and this nurse would not be the last. Because Corrie did not hate but chose instead to love, God used her to spread the message Betsie had described while they were still in the Ravensbruck concentration camp—that no matter how deep the darkness, God was deeper still.[63]

Most of us have not had to deal with pain as great as Corrie's. If God could give her forgiveness and keep her mind from the awful experiences she and her family faced, He can help us focus on Him in the midst of all we face.

"You will keep in perfect peace him whose mind is steadfast, because he trusts in you," Isaiah wrote (Isaiah 26:3). As we repel sin, we do not stand alone. Paul promises us that we have "the mind of

Christ." Jesus' Spirit provides us with a deep under-standing of God's mind and applies that to our lives (1 Corinthians 2:10–16).

Under our own power, we could not alter our thinking. Consider how often we decide in December that we want to lose weight (or make some other permanent change). How many of us have continued to put that decision into action by late February? We get tired of trying to change our thoughts or habits, and in a short time we're in the old rut again.

Paul didn't care if his disciples lost weight, but he did care about their spiritual commitment. He encour-aged the Romans to make themselves spiritual sacri-fices. "Do not conform any longer to the pattern of this world," he told them, "but be transformed by the renewing of your mind. Then you will be able to test and approve what God's will is—his good, pleasing and perfect will" (Romans 12:1–2).

How were new Christians to accomplish this? Paul commands the Colossians, "Set your hearts on things above, where Christ is seated at the right hand of God. Set your minds on things above, not on earthly things. For you died, and your life is now hidden with Christ in God. . . . Put to death, therefore, whatever belongs to your earthly nature: sexual immorality, impurity, lust, evil desires and greed, which is idolatry" (Colossians 3:1–2, 5).

When your heart and mind are spending more time with Jesus than with the world's temptations, your soul will be in good company. Your Christian walk will draw you closer to God, and you will do His will. So "Love the Lord your God with all your heart and with all your soul and with all your mind and with all your strength" (Mark 12:30). With the same intensity you put into your career, your family life, or whatever else is most important to you, put all you have into your spiritual life. Put your focus on Jesus, and don't let sin distract you. That way you won't fail Jesus often or for long, and you'll quickly make it right with Him when you do slip.

But none of us can do this all by ourselves. We all need the support of other Christians.

9

WHAT ABOUT THE CHURCH?

How can other Christians help me know Jesus?

"Whoever does God's will is my brother and sister and mother," Jesus said (Mark 3:35). When you become a Christian, you not only gain God as your Father and Jesus as your Brother, you also get a whole new family of Christian siblings. All those who know Christ are your huge extended family.

As with earthly siblings, sometimes you'll become very close with other Christians, and sometimes you'll wonder how you could possibly be part of the same family. But you are always related by faith to those who have asked Jesus to forgive their sins. When you have troubles, you can turn to a brother or sister for help, and when you need to share joy with someone, another Christian can be there to rejoice with you.

The church should be the Society of the Forgiven and Forgiving.
William George Spencer

In fact, Christians don't live well when they live alone. "Lone ranger" Christianity is not described in the Bible, and it's not part of God's plan. You need other Christians who can help you learn how to draw ever closer to Christ. Even when you've been a Christian for many years, you'll be encouraged and challenged by brothers and sisters in Christ.

Ekklesia: [The Greek word from which we get our word ecclesiastical]...a gathering of citizens called out from their homes into some public place. . . . In a Christian sense, a. an assembly of Christians gathered for worship.[59]

You've become part of the church, a gathering of people called out to live in obedience to God, before the world, showing what it means to know and love Him. That obedience is not designed to be painful (though on occasion you may feel some pain). God promised Israel: "Now if you obey me fully and keep my covenant, then out of all nations you will be my treasured possession" (Exodus 19:5). Imagine that— obedience can make a people treasured by God! It can make *you* a treasured member of His family, too. Jesus promised: "If you obey my commands, you will remain in my love, just as I have obeyed my Father's commands and remain in his love. I have told you this so that my joy may be in you and that your joy may be complete" (John 15:10–11).

All those folks who criticize Christianity never mentioned joy, did they? But any Christian can tell you about it. God didn't design faith in Him to be miserable. Even if you've run into some grim-faced Christians, they probably have moments when they draw close to God and feel the joy of His love. Knowing that Jesus has removed sin gives a Christian happiness and peace the world can never experience. For the first time that person feels really free—free to enjoy God.

May the grace of Christ our Savior,
And the Father's boundless love,
With the Holy Spirit's favor,
Rest upon us from above.

Thus we may abide in union
With each other and the Lord,
And possess, in sweet communion,
Joys which earth cannot afford.

John Newton

When you become part of the Christian family and make Christian friends, you may suddenly appreciate why God calls us brothers and sisters. Before long you may become closer to a Christian than you've ever been to your siblings. Sharing the Christian faith means you share another dimension of life. Knowing Jesus makes you spiritual siblings.

Finding a Church

Maybe you've been fortunate enough to be converted

to Christ from inside a church. You may be getting involved right away, and that's great! Take part in as many growth opportunities as you can. Follow the person who led you to Christ in developing a deep faith, or find someone you can relate to well—perhaps the pastor or a Sunday school teacher who can help you learn more about your new faith.

But if you're not sure that this is the church for you, or if you don't have a clue where to go, that's okay too. Don't just assume you need to go to the closest church—the one around the corner or almost next door. You want to go to the church God has in mind for you. To develop the faith God has given you, you need to develop your own faith walk, work together with the members of a church team, reach out to others who don't know Jesus, and develop close friendships. You may not be able to do that with the church almost next door, but the one on the other side of town or a few towns away might be just perfect.

If, as it was for me when I first met Christ, you haven't been able to jump right into a church, don't be dismayed. You *can* find a vibrant, exciting church that will help you grow.

I became a Christian while I was at college. The

friend who led me to the Lord could hardly believe I'd become a Christian—I'd argued with her so much about her faith that she had finally stopped discussing the subject with me. I accepted Christ all on my own, and when I told her, I doubt she believed I meant it. Just then the church she had been attending had some serious troubles, and she ended up leaving it. So here I was, a brand-new Christian, without anywhere to feed my faith.

I wouldn't recommend the path I took, which was initially to do nothing. True, my options were limited. I didn't have a car and a good church was not in walking distance. But I didn't really seek out anything either. There were Christian groups on campus, but the only one I knew anything about seemed to have a lot of Christians who knew much more about their faith than I did, so I was too embarrassed to attend their meetings, though I desperately wanted to. It was probably a place where I could have grown a lot, but my own fears kept me from it. After about a year, I did tie up with a church, not through a fellow student, but through the maid who cleaned my dorm. But I didn't need to wait that long. I could have started growing much sooner if I'd been willing to risk a little more or look a little harder.

If you don't know where to look, you'll simply have to be brave and take the initiative. If a friend led you to Christ, you may be able to go to the church he or she goes to. If not, begin to pray. God will connect you with a group of Christians. He wants you to share your faith with other people. The Book of Hebrews says: "Let us consider how we may spur one another on toward love and good deeds. Let us not give up meeting together, as some are in the habit of doing, but let us encourage one another" (Hebrews 10:24–25). Sharing fellowship with other Christians keeps your spiritual growth on track.

Perhaps, like a friend of mine who moved to a new town and was looking for a church, you will hear a wonderful local preacher on a Christian radio station. Call and find out about that church. Most pastors will be happy to give you a sketch of what their churches are like. Look in the papers and see what is going on in local churches and what they have to say about themselves. Talk to other Christians and find out about the churches they attend. Check the phone book or visit some Christian websites for the names of local churches. Some churches even have their own websites, with information on services and their ministries.

If you can't find a church right away, but you know someone who is running a Bible study, that may be a good place to start. You may meet people there who have strong churches—and in the meantime, you'll be growing in your Scripture knowledge.

The only way you will know if a church is right for you is to visit it. Do not feel as if a visit commits you to anything, even if some kindly people encourage you a bit too strongly to come again. Remember, you are looking for a church, and just as looking for a job can take time and effort, finding the right church can take more than a single stop.

You may visit a church and find it's not just what you want, but someone at that church may tell you about another congregation that might be more suited to your needs. Some pastors understand that their church is not going to suit every Christian and will be happy to give you ideas about where you might find the church God has in mind for you. Just be sensitive if you bring up this subject. You don't want to offend the pastor or other people. Most people have a strong attachment to their own congregations. Implying that something is wrong is like telling a new mother her baby is ugly!

A Picture of the Right Church

So what do I look for in a church? you may be wondering. A lot of things make up a church relationship, and no one (apart from God) can immediately point you to the correct church for you, but here are a few tips to help you with your search.

Look at a church's Scripture focus

The most important element to look for in a church is how it looks at Scripture. Churches vary widely in how important they think Scripture is: for some it is the most important element; for others it is an important element, but equal with, say, reason or church tradition. For a third type, Scripture has little to say at all. These churches are as likely to look to non-Christian sources for answers to life's big questions as to the Bible.

We may be convinced in our minds of the Bible's authority; we will be even more convinced when we

allow it to have its authority in our lives. We will know for ourselves the experience of God speaking through His written revelation to us. The Bible is God's word, what God has said. He still speaks to us through it today.[60]

As a new Christian, you need a church that puts the Bible at the center of its beliefs. The Bible is *the* book through which we can understand God. Books written by Christians or well-meaning non-Christians cannot provide you with all the answers to every question about God, faith, and morality that you can ask—the Bible can. Because the Scripture "is God-breathed and is useful for teaching, rebuking, correcting and training in righteousness, so that the man of God may be thoroughly equipped for every good work" (2 Timothy 3:16–17), you want to make it the basis of your faith. Here are words of advice, comfort, and teaching that come straight from God's mouth. Could you have a better source for your life?

Make sure the church offers a Bible study

To learn about God and your life in Him, you also need to join a Bible study. If a church does not put a priority on Bible study, it probably will not be one where you can grow in faith. How can you grow if you don't know God's commands to you and the information He wants you to know about Himself? Make sure that the church you join has an active Bible study.

As a new Christian, if your church has an introductory Bible course, a course for new Christians, or a study of one of the Gospels, become involved with that. Many churches have more than one Bible study, and you want one that will focus on the area where you will learn best. If you have questions about which study would be best for you, talk to the pastor or Bible study leader.

Avoid churches that:
- Talk about everything but the Bible.
- Add teachings to Scripture and consider them equal to it.
- Talk about Scripture but never teach you much about it.
- Do not consider Jesus to be God. "Prophet" or "teacher" is not enough.
- Try to separate you from your family and friends (unless there is a real physical or emotional threat

to you). Instead you should be encouraged
to share your faith with them.
• Want to control your entire life.

Look at God's call for you

When you join with a fellowship of Christians, you
want to be able to learn about your faith—what its
most important elements are, as described in the Bible;
how to share it with others; and how you can serve
people in the church and in your world. Naturally, as
a new Christian, there will be areas where you are not
yet ready to serve. Beware of the church that hurries
brand-new Christians into teaching positions before
they know what they believe! But you should have
opportunities within the church and sometimes in
the community to share God's love. Whether that
means helping out with a soup kitchen or lending a
church leader a hand as he prepares a church event,
you should be able to put your faith into action.

Be aware that there is no perfect church

Churches are made up of people, so none are perfect.
All church leaders have disagreements (though some
handle them better than others), and no church is

filled with only loving, amiable folks who agree with you. Once in awhile, God even uses irritating Christians to help you grow! So if you see a problem in a church, don't immediately write it off. Instead, watch how the church handles the problem. If a financial crisis is dealt with in faith, you may have found a great congregation—but if every week the pastor pounds on the members to give more, you may want to move on.

Look for a church where you can become part of the team of believers who are seeking to impact the world for Jesus—then become part of their mission. At times the way the mission is carried out may be a bit fuzzy, but the aim should be clear: This church wants to follow God wherever He wants them to go.

On this earth there will never be a perfect church—though there are many excellent ones. Look for a good church that meets your spiritual needs, but don't condemn a suffering one.

Look for a challenge

The first church I went to after I left college was perfect for young Christians, and many attended there. The level of challenge was designed just for people who had recently come to faith and needed to clean up their lives, through the work of God's Spirit in their lives. While I was there, I grew by leaps and bounds. I began to be sure of what I believed, and I experienced a Christian lifestyle that could carry me through the years.

If you start going to a church that never challenges your lifestyle, perhaps you need to keep looking. God wants you to grow in faith, and that requires a change. Most of us resist change rather than welcoming it, no matter how much we *need* it. Business-as-usual churches are probably more interested in the status quo than outreach for Jesus. Don't settle for the way things are when you can touch the world for God.

Expect to open your spiritual gifts

Did you know that when you accepted Christ, He gave you a "package" of spiritual gifts? These are God-given abilities that you can use for Him—or not use at all, if you are lazy. But in order to be a growing Christian, you'll want to unwrap your package and use what's inside.

Paul talks about these gifts in 1 Corinthians 12 and Ephesians 4:11–13. Naturally you will not be able to take on a pastor's job as a new Christian, but if God puts it in your heart to become a pastor, He will lead you into places where you can develop that gift. As you follow in Jesus' footsteps, your gifts will also grow.

A church that challenges you should also encourage you to live out God's plan for your life. Whether that's praying for hurting people or standing up before the church and giving a testimony of how God changed your life, you can impact others.

In Matthew 28:19–20, Jesus told the apostles, "Go and make disciples of all nations, baptizing them in the name of the Father and of the Son and of the Holy Spirit, and teaching them to obey everything I have commanded you." He didn't mean that only apostles can reach the world. Every Christian has been provided with gifts that could reach all nations; every Christian needs to respond to the command. Spiritual gifts enable you to do that.

How Do I Know I Have the Right Church?

This may seem hopelessly simplistic—but I believe that when you've reached the right church, you will just know it. Perhaps, as was true when I first went to the church for young Christians that I mentioned earlier, you'll have a feeling that you've come home— this is the place for you. God will let you know in some way, whether your heart simply feels a quiet peace about attending this church or you feel more strongly about it. If you do not feel at peace about becoming part of a community, keep praying and seeking. You may go to one church for several weeks, but it may not become the place you need to settle into. Keep your eyes open and keep praying until you feel certain God has this place in mind for you. Choosing a church is a big decision, so take your time if you need to. But each week, make sure you go somewhere. You don't have to join a church to attend for awhile.

Eventually you may feel called to join a church. If you've attended the same place for some time and feel this is where God has called you and will be able to use you, make a commitment to that fellowship of believers. Support the congregation by joining when you are ready.

Growing

Once you've become a Christian and become part of a church, don't figure that your Christian walk can go into low gear. Now is the time to share with others the good news that Jesus died for their sins too. Keep in mind Jesus' commandment to spread the gospel to the whole world, and make sure you tell your friends and family what God has done for you.

But be considerate and sensitive to the feelings of those with whom you share. Perhaps the best way to share will not be with words, but with help—listening to a friend in trouble and counseling her, providing a family in need with money for groceries or a few canned goods. When people see that you care, they are more likely to listen to your words.

Don't barge in on people. If they listen, speak, but if they refuse to listen, simply pray for them until they are ready to hear. Perhaps they need to hear the truth from someone else—you can pray that the right person, you or someone else, will be able to get through.

Knowing Jesus is wonderful. Tell the world in your own way. Now that you've been introduced to Jesus, go introduce Him to someone else!

Suggested Reading and Resources

Lewis, C. S. *The Great Divorce*. A Touchstone Book/Simon & Schuster, 1974. A fantasy about a bus ride between heaven and hell that contains many profound truths about Christianity.

Lewis, C. S. *Mere Christianity*. New York: A Touchstone Book/Simon & Schuster, 1952. A Christian apologetic that focuses on the critical elements of faith.

Munger, Robert Boyd. *My Heart—Christ's Home*. Downers Grove, Il: InterVarsity Press, 1992. An imaginative look at the way Christ comes into the believer's life and makes it new.

McDowell, Josh. *The New Evidence That Demands a Verdict*. Nashville: Thomas Nelson Publishers, 1981. A carefully researched and exhaustive compilation of the arguments against Christianity and how Christians can respond to them.

Strobel, Lee. *The Case for Christ*. Grand Rapids: Zondervan Publishing House, 1998. A journalist's look at the evidence that Jesus is God's Son.

Strobel, Lee. *The Case for Faith*. Grand Rapids: Zondervan Publishing House, 2000. A companion volume to *The Case for Christ*, in which the author looks at the objections to Christianity. Answers the "if God. . .then" questions people pose.

Websites

Here are a few on-line resources that will help you study the Bible, learn more about the Christian world, and connect with other believers.

www.gospelcom.net
www.christianity.com
www.crosswalk.com

Source Notes

[1]Josh McDowell, *The New Evidence That Demands a Verdict* (Nashville.: Thomas Nelson Publishers, 1999), 159.

[2]McDowell, 563.

[3]Stephen Gaukroger, *If You're There, God, I Have a Few Questions to Ask* (Old Tappan, N.J.: Fleming H. Revell Co., 1987), 55.

[4]C. S. Lewis, *Mere Christianity* (New York: Simon & Schuster, 1980), 55–56.

[5]Gaukroger, 45.

[6]McDowell, xxv.

[7]Martin Luther, *Luther's Small Catechism* (St. Louis: Concordia Publishing House, 1986), 48

[8]McDowell, 34, 36.

[9]Information concerning the number of manuscripts available for ancient texts from Steve Kumar, *Christianity for Skeptics* (Peabody, Mass.: Hendrickson Publishers, 2000), 107.

[10]McDowell, 38.

[11]Ken Curtis and Carsten Peter Thiede, eds. *From Christ to Constantine: The Trial and Testimony of the Early Church* (Worcester, Pa.: Christian History Institute, 1991), 36.

[12]E. M. Blaiklock, *Blaiklock's Handbook to the Bible* (Old Tappan, N.J.: Fleming H. Revell, 1980), 165.

[13]Henry H. Halley, *Bible Handbook* (Chicago: Henry H. Halley, 1955), 364.

[14]David Alexander and Pat Alexander, eds. *Eerdmans Handbook to the Bible* (Grand Rapids: Wm. B. Eerdmans, 1983), 474.

[15]From Eusebius, *Church History,* as quoted in Curtis and Thiede, 34.

[16]Lee Strobel, *The Case for Christ* (Grand Rapids: Zondervan Publishing House, 1998), 26–27.

[17]Ibid., 29.

[18]Blaiklock, 168.

[19]Ibid., 173.

[20]Kumar, 110.

[21]*The Revell Bible Dictionary* (Old Tappan, N.J.: Fleming H. Revell, 1990), 575.

[22]Kenneth Barker, gen. ed., *The NIV Study Bible* (Grand Rapids: Zondervan Bible Publishers, 1985), 1591.

[23]Luther, 47.

[24]C. S. Lewis, *Mere Christianity* (New York: Simon & Schuster, 1980), 56.

[25]*The Revell Bible Dictionary* (Old Tappan, N.J.: Fleming H. Revell, 1990, 782.

[26]McDowell, 125.

[27]Alexander and Alexander, 32.

[28]Ibid., 630.

[29]McDowell, 159.

[30]Ibid., 168.

[31]Gaukroger, 57.

[32]For Scriptures in this section I am in part indebted to "Prophecies Respecting Christ," *Torrey's Topical Textbook* as it appears on the Web at www.crosswalk.com.

[33]McDowell, 164.

[34]Strobel, 246–7.

[35]Charles F. Pfeiffer, ed. *Wycliffe Dictionary of Biblical Archeology* (Peabody, Mass.: Hendrickson Publishers, 1973), 65.

[36]Ibid., 265.

[37]For a list of sixty-five prophecies, see *Torrey's Topical Textbook.*

[38]Strobel, 246.

[39]J. A. Thompson, *Handbook of Life in Bible Times* (Carmel, N.Y.: Guidposts, 1986), 26.

[40]Alexander and Alexander, 529.

[41]Strobel, 290.

[42]McDowell, 248.

[43]Luther, 160.

[44]Ibid., 161.

[45]Polycarp, *The Epistle of Polycarp to the Philippians,* Bible Study Tools, *www.crosswalk.com.*

[46]Bruce L. Shelley, *Church History in Plain Language,* 2nd ed. (Dallas: Word Publishing, 1995), 47.

[47]Oswald Chambers, *My Utmost for His Highest,* *www.gospelcom.net/rbc/utmostdevo02–26.shtml.*

[48]Omer Englebert, *Lives of the Saints* (New York: Barnes & Noble Books, 1994), 36.

[49]*The Westminster Shorter Catechism in Modern English* (Phillipsburg, N.J.: Presbyterian and Reformed Publishing Co., 1986), 5.

[50]Chambers, *www.gospelcom.net/rbc/utmost/devo/01–22.shtml.*

[51]*Shorter Catechism,* 5.

[52]Kumar, 101.

[53]M. G. Easton, "Sin," *Illustrated Bible Dictionary* (Nashville: Thomas Nelson Publishers, 1897), under Easton's Bible Dictionary on *www.crosswalk.com,*

[54] From *www.gospel.com.net/chi/HERITAGE/Issuenos/chl027.shtml.* John Newton, Letter VIII, "Letters of His African Hardships and Conversion."

[55]Letter IX, ibid.

[56]Ibid.

[57]Carole C. Carlson, *Corrie ten Boom: Her Life, Her Faith* (Old Tappan, N.J.: Fleming H. Revell, 1983), 135–141.

[58]Ibid., 115.

[59]Joseph Henry Thayer, *Thayer's Greek-English Lexicon of the New Testament* (Grand Rapids: Zondervan Publishing House, n.d.), 196.

[60]Alexander and Alexander, 41.

Inspirational Library

Beautiful purse/pocket-size editions of Christian classics bound in flexible leatherette. These books make thoughtful gifts for everyone on your list, including yourself!

When I'm on My Knees   The highly popular collection of devotional thoughts on prayer, especially for women.
     Flexible Leatherette. $4.97

The Bible Promise Book   Over 1,000 promises from God's Word arranged by topic. What does God promise about matters like: Anger, Illness, Jealousy, Love, Money, Old Age, and Mercy? Find out in this book!
     Flexible Leatherette. $3.97

Daily Wisdom for Women   A daily devotional for women seeking biblical wisdom to apply to their lives. Scripture taken from the New American Standard Version of the Bible.
     Flexible Leatherette. $4.97

My Daily Prayer Journal   Each page is dated and features a Scripture verse and ample room for you to record your thoughts, prayers, and praises. One page for each day of the year.
     Flexible Leatherette. $4.97

Available wherever books are sold.
Or order from:

Barbour Publishing, Inc.
P.O. Box 719
Uhrichsville, OH 44683
http://www.barbourbooks.com

If you order by mail, add $2.00 to your order for shipping.
Prices are subject to change without notice.